Praise for
LEADERSHIP SECRETS / **SHAWN TRAUTMAN**

"Having known Shawn and witnessed his leadership abilities over the last 16 years, I'm glad he decided to share some of his secrets with all of us. Shawn and I worked on many projects together and it was very obvious that his background in leadership combined with his diverse skillset allowed him to excel the way he did. His unique take on things makes this book, and his writing on leadership quite different from any other I've read."

- G. LABANCA (SMALL BUSINESS OWNER / INVESTOR / PARENT)

"In the realm of leadership, few embody the essence of dedication, compassion, and innovation as Shawn does. As a friend, he radiates warmth and support, always ready to lend a listening ear or offer sage advice. As a coach, he instilled both athletic skills and invaluable life lessons of teamwork, resilience, and sportsmanship. As a business consultant, he has been a guiding light, generously sharing fresh ideas and insights that propelled my business forward. Shawn's unwavering support and commitment to excellence make him a true beacon of leadership, inspiring those around him to reach greater heights."

- H. YORK (SMALL BUSINESS OWNER / PARENT)

"Shawn Trautman expresses his first-hand knowledge in an easy to understand way. His writing and teaching are second to none in the area of leadership. Having my own degree in organizational leadership, as well as attending many seminars, I can say this from my own personal experience."

- D. ESSEX (BS, RRT-NPS)

"I worked alongside Shawn as a contractor for the government and I can tell you what he says and writes about is on point. He is very personable and genuine, and that is a key part of his leadership foundation. People naturally follow Shawn, because he engages people as individuals and expresses a genuine interest in each person. He understands that everyone has a story, and he is able to reveal a person's strengths by understanding that person's story."

- S. HINRICHS (BUSINESS CONSULTANT / CONFIGURATION MGMT)

"Shawn is a natural born leader and a motivator, which I have witnessed first-hand. His life experiences have prepared him well to lead, coach and teach as he provides great examples of how to overcome hurdles. This book covers so many aspects of leadership and how to build the skills necessary to compete at high levels. If you want to be a leader, and not just a boss, pay attention to Shawn."

- B. WARNE (VETERAN / AVIATION MECHANIC / PARENT)

"When I was promoted to a leadership role at Disney World (FL), I wanted to become the best leader I never had. To empower my team and have them surpass my achievements. In this quest, I was surprised to discover very few resources that build this mindset... until I found this book—WOW! It embodies the mindset I was looking for. Each chapter has a simple, clear and actionable strategy that I could implement immediately. Also, I was pleased that I had already learned a few of these strategies from my life experiences. The gift I got from listening to the book is that Shawn has a friendly and concise way of expressing those ideas. Shawn is a smart, forward thinking, storyteller that mesmerized me as I listened. His voice is reassuring and clear, making it easy and a pleasure to listen to, and it also conveys the emotions of the point he is making. If you desire to become a better leader at work, in your hobbies, or in your community I highly recommend this book."

- W. HENNINGSEN (FOREMAN AT WDW DISTRIBUTION SERVICES, ORLANDO, FL)

"I've known Shawn for most of my life, thru many stages. Shawn's not only one of the smartest people I've ever known, but Shawn is an innovator. He has a set of gifts and an ability to understand, create, and solve like no one I've ever known. He has an amazing heart, and I couldn't be more proud and fortunate to know him. He's the real deal and knows how to help in so many areas of life."

- C. MCCOY (PHILOSOPHER / SUPPORTER / PARENT / COACH / GURU)

"When you hear someone defined as a good leader, your mind normally assumes something like, oh, they're a great leader in their business, their field of work, or their church. I argue that when you're looking for a true leader, you want someone who challenges themselves to live as a leader... always! Shawn Trautman is that leader. Whether it's working as a teacher or being your best friend, Shawn truly knows how to live the definition of leadership. Shawn has excelled as a leader in both his professional and personal life. As a father he demonstrates leadership to his children, ensuring they have the perfect model to follow. In business he innovates, listens, and has the empathy necessary for all leaders. Shawn Trautman lives the definition of leadership."

- S. ANTONELLI (LCDR, U.S. COAST GUARD / MASTER CRAFTSMAN / ORATOR / PARENT)

"I met Shawn 15yrs ago when dealing with a customer issue at a hotel and the energy that flowed between us was spectacular. I was intrigued and impressed by Shawn's unique take on leadership and problem-solving skills. Together, we resolved the issue, but I took more from our conversation than I could ever have imagined. A+ in leadership to you, sir. Your continuing contribution to the study of human leadership is phenomenal."

- H. MAYHEW (MBA, HUMAN RESOURCES / HOSPITALITY MGMT / TRAINER)

Written by: Shawn Trautman
Published by: Feel Good Books

"THIS BLEW MY MIND. SO MANY GEMS & STRATEGIES I CAN USE IMMEDIATELY."
- J. NELSON (Veteran / Small Business Owner)

LEADERSHIP
Secrets

HOW THE BEST LEADERS THINK DIFFERENTLY
(AND WHAT YOU'RE MISSING)

SHAWN TRAUTMAN

Available in:
Hardcover, Paperback, eBook & Audiobook
wherever books are sold

Published By Feel Good Books, 2025

First Edition, 2025

MANUFACTURED IN THE UNITED STATES OF AMERICA

LIBRARY OF CONGRESS NUMBER 2024902241
LEADERSHIP SECRETS / SHAWN TRAUTMAN

This book is dedicated to the real leaders out there.
The ones leading others in ways that matter—with or without a title.
The ones who foster cultures worth being a part of.

Privately, this list is extensive for me.
Publicly, the following people have inspired me and help others in
meaningful ways—most notably: Dr. David E. Martin, Mike Rowe,
Gary Vaynerchuk, Seth Godin, Jesse Itzler, Oliver Anthony, Robby Starbuck,
Dr. Tom Cowan, Tim Ferriss, Russell Brunson, Steve Bartlett, Vinh Giang,
Jefferson Fisher, John Rich, Jordan Berman, Chalene Johnson, Matt Roeske,
Andrew Godwin, Dr. Lindsey Elmore, Mark Manson, Dr. Henry Ealy,
Jesse Cole, Dr. Dana McGrady, Cole Jennette, Dr. Sabine Hazan,
Vanessa Van Edwards, & Candace Cameron Bure.

And then there are the ones we all know about but rarely see.

I wish you ALL the utmost amount of successes in life!
— With love, respect & gratitude.

FOREWORD

From the moment I met Shawn I knew something was *different about him:*

> *The way he spoke to people.*
> *The way he lit up a room.*
> *The way he listened to those around him.*
> *The way strangers opened up to him.*
> *The way people would follow his lead—but not because he was the one in charge.*

What I've learned over the years is that Shawn is an incredible teacher and has a way of breaking things down that truly connects with people. A big part of his success is directly attributed to the fact that he actually cares whether or not people *"get it."*

With that, he doesn't give up once he starts something—
And him completing *Leadership Secrets* is no different.

In the pages of this book, you'll find more than just words on paper; you'll discover a treasure trove of wisdom, forged through Shawn's countless adventures and profound insights.

But let me tell you—Shawn's writing *isn't* just about giving terms or laying out strategies.

It's about painting vivid portraits of human connection, transformative leadership, and leading in ways that matter.

More than anything, you should know that Shawn is sincere—
And it's one-hundred percent him.

What he put into this book has the potential to completely change the way you view leadership and, hopefully, your ability to lead others in any situation.

Not only is this book broken into bite-sized *"secrets,"* but each one takes you on a journey of transformation.

You'll find yourself thinking about past leaders you've had, times when you've led different groups or teams, and specific instances where a different decision or word could have shifted outcomes significantly.

And, you'll find yourself smiling—at all the new ways of thinking that'll help you the next time you lead others.

That said, let Shawn's journey inspire you to embrace the full potential of leadership and cultivate a spirit of empowerment, authenticity, and compassion in your own life.

It's up to you to unlock the true power to lead—and this book could very well be the key you've been looking for.

Trust me, this book is not just unproven theory—it works in real life. I've been witness to it for more than two decades.

Shawn doesn't just talk the talk—he walks the walk.
And I'm proud to be a part of the team he's built.

I hope you enjoy *"Leadership Secrets"*—and that it helps you in ways you never imagined were even possible.

Best of successes in all you do,

Joanna Trautman

PREFACE

You don't get promoted into becoming a leader—that would be far too easy. No title will ever turn you into someone worth following.

That part—is solely up to you.

And, yes, in an age marked by rapid change and uncertainty, leadership has never been more critical.

Leadership is both an art and a science, a dance between vision and execution, and the relentless pursuit of growth—both personally and organizational.

This book serves as a compass for those navigating the complexities of leadership, offering insights and groundbreaking secrets you won't find anywhere else.

And no, you're not *"perfect just the way you are."* You know it. I know it. *That's why you're here.* That's why people like you and me are out here learning how to get better. We know in our heart of hearts that we *can* and *must* do better for those we serve.

I'm sure of it.

You see, leadership is about inspiring others to rise, to innovate, to create, *AND* to achieve beyond their perceived limits.

It's about fostering a culture where individuals feel valued, empowered, and aligned with shared purpose.

It's about putting your best foot forward, building self-confidence, treating all others with respect and admiration, making mistakes and learning, and holding yourself accountable.

And, it's about *going first.* Taking *the risk.* Starting the *thing.* Having *the talk.* Doing what others don't. Being... *the line leader.*

This is not just a book, it's a journey. You'll find yourself exploring trail after trail as you gather ideas and thoughts in the form of secrets before circling back to camp to incorporate them all. The more secrets you gather and put into your toolkit, the quicker your transformation takes place.

Gone are the days of just showing up and telling others what to do. If you're going to lead others in any form or fashion, show up and truly *give them something to follow.*

Oh, and if you don't care about people, doing what's right, or building something worthwhile, you'll struggle with leadership. You have to want to do better, be better, and show up in a way that means something to those you lead.

And, don't worry, we'll cover each of those and give you ways to improve every aspect of your leadership.

Now, to be clear about this book, it's not the kind of *"Leadership"* textbook most would call *"traditional."* It's not filled with leadership styles, theories, definitions, concepts, and strategies.

Why?

Because all that crap doesn't mean a thing if people don't want to follow you.

And that's important.

This book is about developing the leader inside of you and giving you mindset hacks that'll completely change the way you view yourself *AND* your team.

I'm glad you're here. Together, we can show the world how to lead in a way that makes followers want to follow.

And yes, your future *"you"* needs you… now, more than ever.

I'm Shawn Trautman—and this is my lifelong take on Leadership.
My journey.
My struggles.
My thoughts.
My observations.
My solutions.

My Secrets.

What you need—but won't learn in school.

1

FINDING A WAY

Have you ever driven through fog? You know, like, really dense fog?

The kind of fog where you can barely see ten feet in front of your car. It's awful. And scary. And nerve-racking.

Leadership has these same kinds of moments—regularly.

A brain fog, of sorts. No, not the kind that comes from a lack of coffee (though, that's pretty common).

I'm talking the kind where you don't know the answers.
The kind where you can't see what's in front of you.
The kind where you don't know which way to turn.
The kind where you can't see any good options at all.

You can either give up and say you *"tried,"* or you weather the storm and *"find a way."*

Leaders worth their salt are the ones that "find a way."
And when presented with unfamiliar challenges, they don't give up. Instead, they buckle down and start feeling the feelings.

What feelings?

You know, the feelings you feel when dense fog comes rolling in.

Your heart rate goes up. Your breaths get a little shallower. Nervousness, loneliness, and fear all settle in.

But, something else happens:

> *You become hyper-focused.*
> *You become mindful of things directly in front of you.*
> *You temporarily let go of all those things on the horizon that you can't do anything about—at present.*
> *You get comfortable with the uncomfortable.*

You have to, because you can't see anything else. You have to find a way.

The most important step at this point is to be where you are.
Meaning: be awake. Be alert. Be present.

Being present means you're fully engaged in what you're doing—whether it's a problem you're trying to solve, a conversation, a task, a Zoom call, a board meeting, or in a huddle with your team.

So what happens when you're present? When you're in the zone? When you're deep into the fog?

Your senses become heightened. Your eyes and ears become your guide. What you see. What you hear. You start thinking through the hows and whys of what you're doing like never before.

 **You start building connections and piecing together puzzle pieces you didn't know existed.**

In the background of your mind, you hear Metallica's song, *"Nothing Else Matters"*... but it's faint.

There's mystery in the unknown, and it's part of the allure of leadership.

It's the unconscious incompetence phase... you know—
When you don't know what you don't know.

It's the phase that forces you to have a little hope and faith in the things you can't see or control. It reinforces beliefs that there's something greater outside of what can be seen. It humbles you because you know you don't have the answers or a plan—yet.

To get out of this phase, *you have to trust yourself.* You have to dig deeper and focus, temporarily, on what your next step will be—and then the one after that. And you have to put in the work.

What work?

You read. You search. You watch. You ask questions. You listen. You think. You discuss. You test. You measure. You adjust. You shift. You move. You decide.

You do a lot of things, but what you don't do is give up.

And no, it's not for a grade. It's not to check a box and say:

- ☑ *"Yeah, I completed it,"* or
- ☑ *"I got through it."*

It's not for bragging rights.

It's for the feeling that comes with knowing you're the kind of person that gets it done—that finds a way.

Some people call this persistence. Some, determination. Some call it stubbornness. And some call it being resourceful.

I call it sticktuitiveness. It's *finding a way.*

So maybe...as leaders, let's not be afraid of fog. Let's embrace it, as it allows you to focus and go deep like you rarely get to.

Without fog, you wouldn't engage your super senses. You wouldn't be given the opportunity to make something out of nothing. To make things make sense.

Oh, and there's one more benefit.

Fog allows you to create a vision.
A vision of what could happen next.
A vision of what the landscape will look like when the fog lifts.
A vision of how people will react when you roll out your new program.
A vision of a viable path forward.

And, in perhaps the greatest irony of all, *fog brings clarity—*
Both for you *AND* the people you lead.

But only if you're the kind of leader that finds a way.

SECRET #1

Leadership, much like driving through fog, involves navigating uncertainties and challenges. When faced with the unknown, exceptional leaders don't succumb to despair; instead, they embrace the discomfort, become hyper-focused, and practice sticktuitiveness— the determination to find a way. In the fog of leadership, staying present, trusting oneself, and persistently working through the unknown not only builds resilience but also provides an opportunity to create a clear vision for the future.

2

SUCCESS SPIRALS

What can we discern from the proverbial ladder of success?

What does it really mean? What do the rungs represent? How tall is it? How do we climb? Who came up with the concept—*and why?*

What if...?

What if we changed our thinking?
What if we changed the way we looked at success?

I see the ladder of success as inaccurate and superficial. It's a phrase thrown around loosely, like pennies into a wishing well.

The thing is, the answers are different for everyone. Success is subjective and has no true definition, so it's really an arbitrary point.

Now, instead of a ladder of success, let's think of it as a ladder of growth.

Now, instead of it being a ladder, let's say it's a staircase—
Not just any staircase, but a spiral staircase.

Each step isn't tied to money or rank or title, but instead—growth.

Growth:

>*As a person who learns and adapts to new circumstances.*
>*As a person who gains new skills and makes new connections.*
>*As a person who matures and becomes more reliable and trust-worthy.*

Now, here's where it gets interesting, messy, and thought-provoking. Feel free to join me and step down off the ladder of success you're climbing as I explain the possibilities. You might just stop and look at everything—*and everyone*—a little differently.

Imagine that everyone has their own spiral staircase they're climbing. It's theirs and theirs alone, and there's only room for one person.

Can you picture it?

If not, think of the *"Stairway to Heaven"* image made famous by Led Zeppelin, and then make it a bit more twisted—so that it creates a spiral. Like the **double helix** you once learned about—heck, it's *IN* your DNA.

Okay, good. *"Why the spiral?"* you say. I'm glad you asked.

The spiral is the path each of us takes through the world—
A journey.

When we're infants and toddlers, the steps are small and our base is wide. We take a lot in, slowly, and learn—but we don't look back or down as we're building our foundation.

Some people have a much wider foundation than others.

With each major milestone, a new connection and memory is made. This includes completion of activities as well as sports, graduations, and social experiences. It also includes birthdays, conversations, and any books read.

Step up.

We're all gathering pieces of the puzzle called life and making some kind of *"worldview"* out of it. Authority figures that surround you are your biggest influences at this point—your parents, your teachers, your coaches, respected peers, your heroes, etc.

Step up.

With every new connection you make, you grow a little bit, and your thoughts change. **How you see the world changes.**

Step up.

Before long, your spiral of steps has come ***full circle.*** As a teenager, it happens. You've learned and grown and climbed several steps, completing the circle.

> **Now, looking back and down, you see things from a different perspective.** *The same world—a different viewpoint, if you will.*
> *You think you now "get it," and you do, compared to how you used to think.*

Step up.

Your body is different. Your voice is different. Your hormones are different. Your thoughts are different.

Things you used to care about seem less important. Toys lose their meaning. People that are older don't seem as smart. The world isn't as scary in some ways—and scarier in others.

Step up.

Every interaction in the world is a chance to learn and step. As teenagers, our staircases really start to take shape.

Some people take things slowly, avoid new opportunities, and are not open to learning. Some don't spend much time reading or have open dialogue, and just go about their way without challenging themselves. In fact, they get uncomfortable with changes and want everything to remain as it always was. Their spirals will be long and wide—and will take a long time to ever come full circle.

Step up.

Others will take the *inside track* and step up quickly, while they absorb as much as they can without regard to anyone else. They're learning and growing, but it still takes a while to come full circle.

New realizations help bring it back around.
Perhaps a new relationship or job?

With each new "something," our worldview changes.

The more we experience and reflect on—*and become responsible for*—the more we connect and grow.

Step up.

Growth in the late teens to late twenties is heightened. For a lot of people, this includes being out on their own for the first time. Highlights include making decisions without parents, having real consequences, and making life choices.

Step up.

Now, it starts getting real. Fast.

> New career. *Step up and possibly come full circle.*
> Wedding. *Step up and possibly come full circle.*
> Buy a house. *Step up and possibly come full circle.*
> Have a baby. *Step up and possibly come full circle.*

I say *"possibly"* because sometimes people just step (maybe not even up) and don't stop to look around and see how much their *worldview* has changed.

And, be careful of falling into society's norms—of where you should be, or what you should be buying, or what you should do next. They'll tell you it's what *"everyone who's anyone"* does.

This is you and your journey—

> *Your stairwell.*
> *Your story that's being written right now.*
> *There are no timelines.*
> *There is no race—other than the human race.*

You step when you're ready, not when someone else tells you to.

The more we take on—*that we're willing to understand, think about and truly absorb*—the more we grow and we step higher and higher on our staircase of growth.

Step up.

We mature as we step up and bring things full circle.
We reflect on our past and acknowledge our own mistakes and failures—and take ownership of them so as to not repeat them.

That's growth, in and of itself.
Step up.

As functioning adults, our full circles can now include realizations about parenting, about food, and about health.

It can also include realizations about medicines, about politics, and about others.

Step up.

At each point where we've come full circle, we have the opportunity to look down and see how far we've come—to reflect on older versions of ourselves and to think about how our worldview, once again, is different.

We can also look up, and envision a new future—a different world with new knowledge and experience where we can do things differently or better.

We can also look out and offer assistance to others. Maybe someone is stuck and needs a hand? Maybe someone's stepping down and needs some encouragement?

Step up.

With every step, we have choices. Do we keep stepping up, or do we like the view from here? Do we go back down because we liked it better before? Do we adjust and try to make something different for our futures?

Step up, down, or sideways.

Now, as interesting as this is, we also start seeing others for how they're *moving on* in their lives. Are they stepping up and growing, or are they stepping back down? It doesn't make us better or worse—but it helps us understand our own journeys, and who'll be there with us.

One more twist to this.

To live a well-balanced life, everything that makes you *"you"* has to step up when you're ready—and it all has to come full circle at the same time. Realizations in our lives affect everything about our lives—good, bad, or indifferent.

That said, it's important we take care of ourselves *mentally, physically, and spiritually.*

 **Growth stops when we stop stepping—**
When we're no longer interested in learning or going new places or meeting others.

And—learning isn't a "school" thing, it's a mindset.
It has nothing to do with grades.

Learning can happen anywhere, at any time, and from anyone—
Don't ever forget that.

When nothing changes, nothing changes.

At some point, though, most people will start stepping down.
As we step down, we let go of responsibility.
We let others do as they need to without taking ownership of it.
We cut back to a bare minimum—*a downsizing of sorts*—until we're once again comfortable.

At this point, we can look back up and celebrate where we once were, what we once had, and the experiences we were a part of.

We can also look back at the trips we took, the conversations, money, etc.
We can smile and be proud—or we can choose to start stepping again.

Learn from your mistakes, but don't beat yourself up over them.

Life's about choices. And attitude. If you want to grow and step up, expect that the world will soon look different to you. The way you see others will change. Others will change as they go, as well. People everywhere are out stepping on their own staircases and some will outstep you. And others will get tired and just... stop.

It's okay. It's their journey.
Live yours.

Keep stepping until you can't, but always take the time to look back and down—and pat yourself on the back for how far you've come.

You're the only one that knows your journey inside and out. Use it as your _stepping stones,_ and push yourself to your own _personal high._

I believe in you.

Oh, and one last thing.

Be careful of _elevators_—you know, circumstances that bring us new highs and lows, quickly. Sometimes, we don't know which direction we're going nor which floor we'll get off on.

Things like:

>_Being promoted too quickly,_
>_Coming into a lot of money overnight,_
>_Major accidents,_
>_Abrupt ends to relationships,_
>_Unplanned pregnancies,_
>_Death of friends or a loved one._

We'll all experience different versions of these at some point in our lives—and we have to be careful to **NOT** take the elevators. The fall is much too hard.

Take the necessary *steps* to learn, even if they're steep.

The phrase ***"spiraling out of control"*** could easily have a new meaning based on this mindset. Are you seeing it?

So, to summarize: perhaps we should stop calling it a ladder of success?

It's your own personal staircase of growth—with beautiful spirals.
Yours is what you make it.
And so is mine.

Step up, down or sideways, just keep stepping.

Life's a continuous journey—
And it changes with every step you take.

SECRET #2

The traditional concept of the "ladder of success" is misleading and superficial. Instead, we should view it as a personal "staircase of growth," with each step representing individual learning, adaptation, and maturation. The metaphor of a spiral staircase emphasizes the continuous, evolving nature of personal development, with the opportunity to reflect, learn and grow at every turn, ultimately challenging the conventional notions of success and encouraging a more personalized, mindful approach to life's journey.

3

RESILIENCE

R esilience.

Officially defined as:
"The capacity to recover quickly from difficulties; toughness."

But what is it, really?
And, why is resilience so important to our own well-being?

Perspectives, failures, injuries, successes, and cancel cultures are all affected by our resilience—so let me unpack it a bit here.

Resilience.

Hearing, seeing, feeling, smelling, or tasting something that isn't your norm—*or your preferred thing*—gives you the opportunity to expand your horizons. It also allows you to better understand a different perspective or *thing* you wouldn't ordinarily partake in.

Each one builds your resilience.

Canceling something because it's not what you're used to, want, know about, or prefer breaks down your resilience.

Resilience means you learn to accept failures, dislikes, language you don't use, foods you don't eat, approaches you don't use, and cars you despise.

Resilience becomes just part of the world you live in—and not something you are *triggered* by.

When someone is *triggered,* it's usually stress- or trauma-related. Stress is something we all have and live with, and learning to *roll with the punches* instead of *crashing and burning* has much to do with one's resilience.

Resilience.

> **Building resilience happens over time.** *Resilience is a combination of self-awareness, optimism, self-care, problem-solving skills, and a belief in one's abilities. Resilience is also a strong and healthy social support system, self-control, empathy and coping mechanisms.*

When someone uses a colloquialism, you could ask questions, smile, have a puzzled look, laugh in a good way, try to figure it out, or just say, *"Poof, be gone!"* to make yourself feel better.

When someone uses foul language, you have an option to tune in, try to understand the context, dismiss the language completely, get offended, or say, *"Poof, be gone."*

When someone says or does something that makes you uncomfortable, you have an option to sit back and watch body language, listen for intent, ignore the situation outright, be appalled, or say, *"Poof, be gone."*

By canceling others using the *"Poof, be gone!"* strategy, you risk developing a very sensitive, thin-skinned approach to the world. By doing this, you end up with a well-earned *fragile* sign stamped across your forehead.

Some might even replace that with a snowflake sign and it would be just as fitting.

Resilience.

Resilience isn't built from pleasing everyone and/or just removing things, people, food, etc. from existence.

Resilience says you're okay with others—with others' choices, with others' beliefs, with others' likes, with others' dislikes, with others' smells—and that you're okay with yourself.

Resilience says you're mindful of your surroundings and your emotions, and that you understand the importance of gratitude.

Resilience is built around diversity. The more diverse your environment is, the more resilient you are to differences in opinion, likes, choices, disappointments, and successes.

The more you realize that *YOUR* truth is often fluid and based on your current understandings—and that *YOUR* truth may not be someone else's—the more you're open to understanding others while connecting dots.

Resilience.

Being disappointed regularly is also important in the quest for resilience as *you have to learn to control your emotions* before they control you.

Salespeople thrive on *"NOs,"* so they don't take it personally and can get to overcoming objections.

A no is simply a yes to something else. *NO* can also mean, *"New Opportunity."*

Having successes, regularly, is just as important in the quest for resilience, as you have to learn to control your emotions before they control you.

Promotions, windfalls of money, new jobs, awards, winnings of any sort—they all affect how one thinks and acts.

Success often alters the ego and can have detrimental effects on others around us if it's not understood and trained.

Handling success comes with responsibilities that must also be handled with grace and gratitude.

Knowing how to change your perspective and move past any obstacles or unexpected win is an important life strategy.

Persistence is built from a person who won't take no for an answer, or an athlete who won't stop practicing until they hit a particular goal, or a marketer who doesn't stop testing ads until one hits a particular click-through rate.

Resilience.

Resilience says:

> *You can get knocked down eight times, and you get up eight times.*
> *It says you can act like Teflon and don't let anything stick to you.*
> *It says you can take a beating on the front lines at work and still show up the next day with a positive attitude, as though nothing ever happened.*
> *It says you can handle adversity and learn to stick and move as situations around you change.*

It says you can handle going without something because you know what it means to go without.

Perhaps we should all stop removing friends or family from our lives because you just can't *"deal"* with them.

Perhaps we should accept differences, listen for context and for understanding, and then merely put it in our *"how to deal with people"* arsenal and move on.

Learning to detach—*emotionally and spiritually*—is key for many folks, as the detachment allows for a much-needed separation from the situations and people that created it.

Prayer, meditation, support groups, and therapy are a few of the available solutions that are widely used.

Resilience.

You see, there's way more we all will like about each other if we focus on finding similarities instead of trying to cancel anyone who has differences.

And, by the way, everyone's different from you.

Canceling others says you have no interest in ever seeing or hearing someone again because they say or think something different than you, and that's just asinine.

Sure, you get to choose, but choose wisely.

If you know, up front, that we're all different, we all learn from each other.

If you actively seek out and talk only to people who are very much like you, you'll have no chance at being resilient.
Resilience.

And, no, I'm not saying we should accept bad behavior or being mistreated emotionally, physically or other—that's not the same as just a *difference.*

We all need to have an *"enough is enough"* point and not allow our tolerance level to become *the new normal* as it's a slippery slope that goes fast.

And, last, it's okay to remove toxic people from your lives and it's okay to blatantly call out actions from others that are simply not acceptable.

In fact, I'd dare say it's recommended.

Resilience.

If you want to be an effective leader, you'll need a healthy supply of resilience to draw from.

And *YES,* it's much more than what the official definition would lead you to believe.

SECRET #3

Resilience is not just about recovering quickly from difficulties but encompasses a mindset that embraces diversity, accepts differences, and finds strength in facing challenges. It emphasizes the importance of building resilience over time through self-awareness, optimism, self-care, problem-solving skills, and maintaining a healthy social support system, all of which contribute to a more balanced and mindful approach to life.

4

DELEGATION VS. EMPOWERMENT

Delegation vs empowerment... at home and at work.

Being a leader *isn't the same* as being a manager.

Managing people *isn't the same* as being a leader.

Being a leader means someone's following you—
Regardless of your job title.

True leaders create a following, but not because they're in charge.

And, having **followers** has nothing to do with leading—but they **can** work hand in hand.

Okay, so to the main topic: **delegation vs. empowerment.**

I had a great conversation the other day with a friend of mine who's in a leadership position in the Coast Guard. Afterwards, I thought through the topic much further and wrote down my key points to come back to.

Ultimately, it's this:

Leaders empower others while managers delegate tasks.

As a parent, if you're merely **_TELLING_** your kids what to do, you're delegating tasks.

> *"Take out the garbage!"*
> *"Clean your room!"*
> *"Pick up the living room!"*
> *"Do the dishes!"*
> *"Go get me a beer!"*

The list goes on and on. It's task-oriented. It's about compliance: *"I don't want to do this and, since I'm in charge of you, I get to tell you to do it."*

This is the lowest form of leadership as it's really more about being a task manager. You get to decide what needs to be done and you assign it to someone you think should do it.

Yay! Just like that, you're a leader!

Sorry, but, it doesn't work like that.

 **_Busy work doesn't make people better—it merely passes time._** I've had many teachers and managers in the past give me busy work that has no real purpose other than to get through something without having to think.

Internships often abuse this and hire interns to simply be gophers. Gopher is also broken down as *"Go For"*—meaning: *go for coffee*, or *go for bagels*, or *go for this* or *go for that*.

Being a gopher often leads to resentment, although the manager of said gopher often feels like they're doing a great job of **"leading."**

Again, not the case.

Formal authority—aka formal power, legitimate power, or positional power—is when someone has authority over you and can tell you what to do. A boss. A parent. A teacher. A fire chief. A CEO. A captain.

If you're directed to do something from someone with formal authority, refusal to do so can result in termination of your job. If it's a parent, you risk whatever means of punishment the parent sees fit—grounding, spanking, loss of *something*, etc.

Leadership is earned.

Delegating does not improve one's leadership skills nor does it garner respect from the person being told what to do...regardless of how nice that person is being.

Delegation creates a "what do I do next?" mentality and a "no one told me what to do so I didn't do anything," kind of a mindset.

This is very limiting. And frustrating.

Empowerment (also called Entrusting) is a transfer of power from one person to another. Often, someone with some type of legitimate power will look to enable or entrust another person by getting them to **think, act, and fail** on their own in order to grow.

As a parent, this is critical if you want successful kids in the long run.

As a boss, this is critical *if you want your employees to grow within the organization or outside of the organization later on.*

It even works with friends or co-workers as the aim is to literally make someone else better or more confident or less dependent on others in some way.

Here's the tough part though, especially for parents:

> *By the nature of what it is, when you empower someone, their dependence on you goes down.*
> *When they depend on you less and less, your power over them goes down.*
> *The more they 'get' on their own, the greater their independence, and the more they can do for themselves.*

Differently, their loyalty goes up.

And, as a parent, this is both great and awful. It's great because they become the best version of themselves, and they're not afraid of what life throws at them. At the same time, it's awful because the person you've spent such a long time 'working with' no longer needs you the way they once did.

A lot of people struggle with this.

Empowerment is truly a transition of power with the priority on the recipient.

Empowerment is a transfer of understanding—hows and whys are critical. It emphasizes importance and relevance. It often comes with learning new skills, and when and how to apply them. It's learning one lesson at a time until an entire collection of lessons is known and thought through with critical thinking. It's enabling others to think their way through situations.

Here's a great example.

I recently shared some pictures of my fourteen-year-old son who, in one of the pictures, was greasing one of the many tractors he works on. Then there was an action shot of him running one, and another of him disconnecting some electrical wires, and clearing drywall. He wasn't told what to do—and then miraculously **get it** by doing. He's learned over the years. Does he understand the importance of grease points? Yes. Does he understand when and why to keep them greased? Yes. Does he know how to use and perform a wide variety of skills on multiple machines? Yes. Does he know the importance of respirators and how to use them? Absolutely.

The list goes on. But, it wasn't done all at the same time. You don't empower someone with a single moment. It happens slowly, as understanding grows. It's gradual and comes with lots of little connections.

It's how I've run my businesses. It's how I teach my classes. And it's how I've raised my kids.

My goal is to empower, not to tell someone what to do.

> ***Believe in them and tell them so—until they end up believing in themselves enough to make positive changes on their own.***

Ever since my near-death experience over a decade ago, my goal is to make people around me ***self-sufficient*** in as many different ways as possible.

So, how can you tell the difference?

Delegation is focused on the person who's telling someone what to do —as *THEY* get the benefit.

"*Do this for me and you won't get punished.*"

> *"I'm in charge and I want this done so I can look better by saying I got you to do it."*
> *"I don't want to do this and I'm in charge of you so you do it."*
> *"Do it now because I said so."*

You know, those kinds of things.

Empowerment is focused on the person doing the job—

> *Do you have everything you need to be successful?*
> *Do you understand why I'm having you do this?*
> *Can you tell me the steps you'll need to do the next time this happens?*
> *If I'm not here next time will you know how to take action?*
> *If I leave you in charge can I be assured you can handle anything that comes up?*

With kids, it's easy to just simply tell them what to do—

> *It doesn't mean they're learning anything by doing so.*
> *It doesn't get them to think.*
> *It just means they'll comply.*
> *It just makes them resentful.*

With employees, having every task laid out and measured doesn't allow for any stretching or improvement.

It just says, *"I basically need a robot and I need you to do only this— nothing more."*

You see this all the time with employees that can't make up their mind or make decisions.

> *"I'm sorry, I'll have to ask my boss,"* or
> *"I'll see if I can get the manager to help you in some way,"* or
> *"I'll let the manager know, and they'll get back to you,"* or

"I'm sorry, there's nothing I can do," or worse,
"I'm sorry, I wish I could do something to help."

The more each one of us becomes empowered—
The more everyone around us wins.

We become responsible for decisions and thus think through the ramifications of choices—rather than tossing it over to someone else.

Parents, empower your children and watch them flourish. You'll all be better off in the future as you'll be able to treat them as functioning adults rather than taking care of them forever.

Managers, empower your employees and watch them **outgrow** their positions. You'll change the lives and futures of those who work for you—and make them feel like they work **with** you.

If you've done it right, your past employees will go on to grow in all they do and even run their own successful organizations.

It's tough, but it's the right thing to do.

Look for ways to empower people around you and you'll benefit as well.

Limit others, and you'll always feel like you're the only one that can do anything—and you'll burn out over time.

The next time you're given the option of how to lead, ask yourself this question:

Am I helping someone become better at something, or am I
merely having someone do something for me?

If you're empowering others, you're using your candle to light other candles that may eventually burn brighter than your own.

You're becoming the leader you've always wanted to be. You'll grow just by watching others grow—and, I'll warn you now, it's addicting.

Be the one who empowers others and feel better about your contribution to the world, as it'll have ripple effects.

Don't be selfish and hold people back just so you'll have someone to do the dirty work you don't want to do.

Oh, and empowering the wrong person can backfire quickly—as they'll abuse the newfound power and use it against you.

Empowering someone with inherent character flaws can—*and often will*—create a monster. You basically amplify characteristics that need not be amplified, so don't just do this blindly.

Empowerment is often a direct result of good leadership.

If you're able to cultivate an environment that produces strong leaders all around you, you've done a remarkable service to the world—and should be commended.

SECRET #4

True leadership lies in empowerment, not delegation. Leaders empower others by fostering independence, encouraging critical thinking, and facilitating personal growth. Managers who merely delegate tasks may gain compliance, but miss the opportunity to develop true leadership skills and build a loyal, empowered team.

5

COMMUNICABILITY

How you communicate matters.

I recently took ownership for a communication mishap that'll serve as the basis for this chapter.

Here's what went down.

A friend of mine was staying at a hotel where we were to go fishing. We were to catch the boat off the back loading area behind the hotel's restaurant at 6am.

At 5:30 in the morning, I called to ensure he was up and going. No answer. I then went to the front lobby of the hotel and asked the front desk guy to call his room. He did. Again, no answer. I tried his cell again, no answer.

6am came and went, and still no friend. He was legit about to **miss the boat.** I knew he had no transportation as a friend had dropped him off so I made a different call.

At 6:15, as the boat was about to pull out I had them wait so I could drop off the keys to my truck at the front desk with a note for him when he came down.

To ensure he got the message, I called him again and left a detailed voicemail about what was going on and where the keys were.

Fast forward ten hours when the boat came back in. I saw several text messages from my friend saying he was some fifteen miles north, had taken a bus, and then an Uber, and that he was now walking to some other store.

Confused, I went to the hotel lobby and asked about my keys. Yep. They were still there with the note and the lady said, *"He never showed up."* I thanked her and then set off to find him.

Forty-five minutes later I tracked him down and questioned what had happened. He was now confused.

I said, *"Why didn't you take my truck?"*

He said, *"You didn't give me the keys."*

It occurred to me right then and there that I'd made a mistake. *Not him.*

And that's the point.

I take complete responsibility for accurate and thorough communications. At the time I thought what I'd done was enough. I called over and over and took action **AND** left him a voicemail with a detailed plan of attack.

Here's the lesson:

> *I've communicated with this guy countless times via the phone and through text messages. By doing what I did, I violated the **first rule** in communicating effectively.*

What's the rule?

 ***Always communicate in the native platform of the person you want to receive your message.***

In other words, if it's important for me to get my message to you, then I need to use the platform **YOU'RE** most comfortable with… not me.

If you use Messenger and I want you to see something, I'll send it in Messenger. Most people don't care, but I do.

If I want my message to get to you, I want to give it the best possible chance.

If you only respond via Instagram messaging, then that's where I'll go. If you use text messages as your go-to, then I should know that and use text messaging.

In this case, I had no idea he'd never set up his voicemail nor does he know how to use it. He said it wasn't my fault but I knew better.

Truth is, I should have kept the conversation in the place where I know he communicates.

And, this is the lesson for all of us.

If someone uses only email, don't send them a text. If they only check Messenger every month or so and you need a response today, it's not good enough to send them a message there and then just sit back and wait.

When our message is important enough to send, the next question should be:

> *"What's the best way to get this message to them in their preferred platform?"*

If it's text—send a text.
If it's SnapChat—send a snap.
If it's on Instagram—go there.

It was me. *I made the mistake.*
I owned it. *I took the blame.*
I apologized. *I learned the lesson.*
I made it right. *I got better.*

So, yeah—how you communicate matters.

SECRET #5

Effective communication involves understanding and utilizing the recipient's preferred platform. Taking responsibility for a communication mishap, the importance of choosing the right medium is emphasized, acknowledging that effective communication is not just about the message but also about the method of delivery tailored to the recipient's comfort zone.

6

WHEN IS ENOUGH ENOUGH?

When is enough enough?

Perhaps you've always dreamed of collecting something? Cars. Money. Paintings. Baseball cards. Jewelry. Collecting for the sake of collecting. More of this. More of that. More than anyone else. At some point, you must ask yourself:

When is enough enough?

Accepting less than desirable conditions at home or work is often considered a means to an end. Poor communication. Crap work. Getting yelled at. Long hours. Lopsided responsibilities.

We all have choices as to what's acceptable—and what's not—and we have to speak up for ourselves. But, we have to have clearly defined limits and boundaries to help provide framework for the question:

When is enough enough?

Addictions come in all shapes and sizes. Smoking. Alcohol. Porn. Drugs. Technology. Sex. Gambling. Racing. Exercising.

Recognizing patterns and acknowledging it for what it is is critical—and so is knowing your limits. As in:

When is enough enough?

Life comes at us fast. It's easy to get wrapped up in the thing that provides you comfort for the moment. It's hard to see the wake or trail you leave behind when you're only looking forward.

> *When we're able to set limits, we protect not only our own well being—but the well being of those around us.*

The next time you find yourself falling into that same old routine and putting your own wants and desires ahead of everyone else at everyone else's expense ask yourself:

When is enough enough?

Decisions from that point forward are better managed, respectful of others, and far greater than those that are just self-serving.

And yes, this question applies to dealing with others:

> *People you lead. People you follow. Businesses you frequent. Community leaders. Politicians. Celebrities. School administration. Friends. Family members. Neighbors.*

When is enough ENOUGH?

SECRET #6

Recognizing and establishing limits is crucial in various aspects of life. Whether dealing with personal desires, work conditions, addictions, or interactions with others, asking the question "When is enough enough?" prompts self-reflection, better decision-making, and consideration for the well-being of oneself and those around us.

7

MUTUAL RESPECT

'll never forget the day it happened.

I was about to graduate from UCF in Orlando, and working as a server at Tony Roma's on I-Drive. I absolutely loved my job as I got to meet tourists every day and had the best time with my guests. I was never the fastest server, but I was memorable and I had several write-ups from guests that were so good that they made it all the way up to corporate.

Then, one day, I came in and we had no bussing staff—no one to bus the tables. Typically there were either two or three guys and probably twelve to fifteen servers. *Everyone was asked if they were willing to take it on but no one accepted as it was less pay and considered crap-work.*

I spoke up and said I'd do it.

Within minutes, I'd taken my server get-up off and had put on a white apron-like thing to keep from getting dirty dishes all over me. Then, I was off and running as there were dirty tables everywhere and servers waiting around for me to get them cleaned.

It was 1999 and times were a little different, but not really. At first, I felt like I was going to be celebrated for **saving the day.** I thought, for sure, everyone will be thankful and I'll be heralded as a hero. As the day progressed, my perspective changed.

I thought my job was merely to clean and clear tables, but it was so much more. Not only was I carrying a large tray full of dirty dishes, I was also picking up trash from the floors, cleaning the men's room, cleaning the ladies room, replacing silverware, cleaning and brewing coffee, filling up empty drinks, cleaning and resetting each table, running orders out to guests, and bringing out salt, pepper, napkins, ketchup, A1 and mustard more times than I can count.

During the course of the six-hour shift I saw, firsthand, what I'd never seen before. Complete and utter disrespect. Prejudice against me based on my position. ***Being ignored and talked down to, constantly, by co-workers.*** And, perhaps the worst part... Being told by guests to *"go away"* as they didn't want me around their table or even talking to them—happened twice.

Never. Have. I. Ever.

I couldn't believe that I had been there on a daily basis for a year and a half and never noticed anything even **REMOTELY** close to this. The next day I spoke to the regular bus boys—*both were hispanic*—and they told me it happens to them **ALL THE TIME** and they just ignore it.

Well, I couldn't.

I was appalled and made it a point from that day on to never talk down to anyone based on their job or for anything I merely **perceive as the truth.** I was ashamed of being a part of the system that these guys felt was just **"how it is."** I'd like to believe I never did those things or spoke down to them in any way, but I honestly don't know because it wasn't on my radar.

And that was the day it fully connected with me. So let me sum it up by slowing down my thoughts and saying it a bit more clearly:
Your position does not make you a better human being than anyone else. Ever.

Your position is merely what was assigned to you (warranted or not) and something you accepted.

For those who look down on others, do know that there are lots of others who see it. For those of you who are in positions that often get mistreated (janitors, host/hostesses, lunch ladies, bus drivers, secretaries, bus boys, etc.), hold your heads high and know your own worth. This world is full of people willing to beat you down mentally and you've gotta keep going.

For now, I'll keep showing up and doing what I do because it matters and I know I can make a difference. I might even look to pick up a shift or two as a bus boy just to be reminded of how important it is to always treat the little guy (or gal) as an equal.

And, to be honest, those are the people I've come to respect and admire more than the ones at the top. Mutual respect for all others is critical. Treating people like they matter regardless of their position cannot be emphasized more.

As leaders, we have to understand this up and down the chain.
We also have to watch out for our teams and ensure everyone understands this concept.

Last, don't be afraid to jump in and help out on the front lines. Often, this is one of the best places for leaders to see how things really work and how the rest of their team behaves.

SECRET #7

One's position or title does not determine their worth as a human being, and the way people are treated often reveals more about those in positions of authority than those in subordinate roles. Worth, dignity, and respect for all individuals, regardless of their job or role, is crucial for a healthy and supportive community.

8

BUILDING LOYALTY

W hat is loyalty anymore?

You see it all the time. Every major company. Grocery stores. Coffee Shops. Websites. Credit cards.

Loyalty used to mean something.

It used to be something that was earned over time—
Not something you bought into.

It was something where you knew the owners of a store or the employees and you shopped there because they meant something to you.

You knew how much your business meant to them, and you trusted them to take care of you.

Loyalty went both ways.

You knew, *as a consumer,* that they were looking out for you—
And you rewarded them with your business.

They knew, *as a business,* that you were looking out for them—
And they rewarded you with customer appreciation 'rewards' that meant
something.

You demonstrated your loyalty by:

> *Showing up,*
> *Telling others about your experiences, and*
> *Choosing **them** over other competitors.*

They demonstrated their loyalty by:

> *Treating you like family,*
> *Welcoming you by name,*
> *Thanking you for being there, and*
> *By building a long-term relationship with you—because you truly*
> *mattered.*

You didn't need a rewards card to get a discount.

You didn't need a cold reminder that flashes in front of you that says, *"Thank you loyal customer."* You didn't have to look up your account to see if you're reward eligible.

I recently went to a Lowe's and had to check myself out as there was only self-checkouts. Everything was computerized. Not a soul in sight.

Contrast that with me walking into my local ACE Hardware and getting welcomed by my first name and having the owner walk and talk with me all the way through when I checked out.

I have fifteen **Loyalty Rewards** cards in my wallet, but there's not a single one of them that I'm actually loyal to. They're all gimmicks to make me feel **better** at the moment of purchase.

> **Loyalty won't get better with AI.**
> *It won't increase with computerized systems. It won't strengthen my relationship with the store. It won't get me to brag on the people.*

The word **Loyalty** has been overused by marketers in such a way that people are desensitized. Most people overlook the word and don't even think about it anymore. It's merely to get something quickly and not actually about being loyal.

But, what if?

> *What if loyalty programs were the focus of businesses again?*
> *What if business owners took the time to ask questions and truly get to know their customers?*
> *What if employees had an incentive to create relationships?*
> *What if they were taught how to cultivate experiences and they understood the value in the customer's eyes?*
> *What if they went out of their way to do things for customers that truly meant something?*

I'll tell you what if... Things would be different.

Businesses are not cold, data-driven entities that are solely focused on making more money while cutting expenses. Businesses are made up of real people who depend on others to make things happen. Businesses depend on their employees, their business relationships, and on their customers.

So why do most employees feel like there's no loyalty towards **THEM?** **Huge problem, right?**

If companies can't even be loyal to their employees, what makes you think they care about you, at all?

Leaders, pay attention—

There's a major opportunity here that shouldn't be overlooked. If you get it right, your company culture changes, your employee retention changes, and your customers actually start becoming **loyal.**

Loyalty starts at the top *and has to work its way down to the bottom.*

Every leader, manager, associate, front line employee and customer should **FEEL** the loyalty and be willing to reciprocate.

If it's not there from the company, it won't be there from the employees.

And if the employees within the business don't care, you can bet the Loyalty Rewards Program will fail over time.

Short-term profits over long-term relationships is a losing strategy.

You want loyal customers?

> *Start by truly caring about those you serve. For businesses, you serve your **employees** as well as your **community**.*

Focus on loyalty and you'll end up with it.

SECRET #8

In the modern era, loyalty has lost its genuine essence, becoming a mere transactional gimmick across various industries. Once a reciprocal relationship built on trust and personal connections, loyalty has been diluted by impersonal rewards cards and automated systems. The true secret lies in rediscovering loyalty's core values, where businesses prioritize genuine connections, personalized service, and mutual commitments between customers and employees. The key to reviving loyalty is not through AI or technology but through businesses embracing a culture where loyalty starts from the top, trickles its way down through every level, and ultimately flourishes in long-term, meaningful relationships with customers.

9

THE BALANCING ACT

Ebb and flow, yin and yang, give and take, plus and minus, positive and negative, left and right, increase and decrease, see and saw, up and down, work and play, clean and dirty, win and lose, light and dark, fire and water.

Do opposites attract or are they necessary to maintain balance and an equilibrium of sorts?

When we have imbalances of forces, in almost every type of environment—something suffers, or degrades.

Food, power, money, commodities, land, supplies, corruption, water, oil, relationships, fisheries, economy, chemicals, etc.

Too much of a good thing is a bad thing.
Too much of a bad thing is usually worse.

The more we take, the more someone else loses.
The more we give, the more someone else takes.
The more we work, the less we play.
The more we worry, the less we enjoy.

The trick is to find balance somewhere in your life and to work to maintain it. Then another, and another, and so forth. Control what you can, in fact, control or influence and let go of the others.

As time goes on, everything requires maintenance as the unbalancing occurs and we have to work to regain it. If not, everything starts feeling like it's weighing us down and eventually feels insurmountable without intervention.

Feeling *"weighted down"* can easily be a result of cortisol as it floods your body. Anger, stress, fear, anxiety, and guilt can all contribute here and disrupt your body's chemical balance point.

It's times like these where it's easy to freeze and do nothing but wallow in self-pity. Analysis paralysis sets in. Try to recognize when this is happening and work to rebalance.

To balance yourself chemically, you have four natural **feel-good** chemicals to choose from. The best part is that releasing them is mostly in your control.

What are they?
I thought you might ask.

The first is dopamine.

When released, it's a shot of happiness. Anything that gives you pleasure releases dopamine. It could be exercise, dancing, cooking, shopping, listening to music, or even something like completing a small task at home or at work. Each time you do something you love or complete something, you release dopamine.

The second is oxytocin.

This is a hormone your body naturally produces when you have skin-to-skin contact. Hugging, kissing, touching, holding hands, massages, cuddling, sexual intimacy—they all release oxytocin. This is why hugs, real genuine hugs, can feel **SO** good—even after they end. It's really just that body contact releases oxytocin **AND,** there's a bonus here—it helps both parties.

Next is Serotonin.

This one is really good for your immune system and is associated with happiness, focus, and calmness. Things like gratitude, meditation, and mindfulness all help release it. Sunlight and sleep help produce and release it and so does positivity. Positivity can happen through events, thoughts, books, conversations, and accomplishments—think awards ceremonies, a viral video you create, or, perhaps, a product release.

And last, but just as important as the other three, are endorphins.

Producing endorphins is a result of pain from something, generally physical. It's a high that comes from things like a long run, a heavy workout, an intense dance session, or even a super cold shower or dip in a frozen lake after you get used to it for a short period. A few other things that release endorphins include laughing, acupuncture, and eating chocolate.

Yes, chocolate!

Each of the four natural **happiness** chemicals can combat and **balance** the stresses of everyday life and the overwhelming feelings we all get.

Again, it's important to keep all these in check.

Leaders, taking an active role in caring for the foundational things in your life is a great first step—

Health (both physical and emotional),

Food,
Sleep,
Relationships,
Finances.

An **imbalance** of any one of these things will leave every other area of your life vulnerable and on shaky ground.

And, believe it or not, making sure your team understands these things and is taking care of themselves matters. You have to rely on them as well and it's important to look after their well-being and not just your own.

The lesson here is that life is not one-sided and needs balance.
Find a balance point and then work to find another.

The good and bad news is there will never be balance in every area of your life at the same time. Once you learn this, you get to choose what gets your attention.

Find your balances—and enjoy more out of life.

SECRET #9

There's an inherent duality and balance in life, expressed through a myriad of opposites. There's a profound truth that equilibrium is essential, both in the natural order and within oneself, emphasizing the delicate harmony required to navigate the complexities of existence. The takeaway is an invitation to actively seek and maintain balance in various aspects of life, understanding that the interplay of opposites is not just a cosmic dance but a practical guide to well-being, both mentally and physically.

10

BOSS MOVES

You're the boss, right?

I mean, if you're the boss, the buck stops here. You get the say. You're the leader. The one who makes the decision and that's that. Everyone knows that when it's time to take action, you're the person to do it.

And, that's great, because you know all the answers. As the boss, you must, right? People depend on you. Bills have to get paid. Money has to flow. Items have to be bought. Paperwork has to be completed. Tests have to be graded. People have to be disciplined.

Someone has to be responsible:

> _Perhaps you have a staff of folks that all get paid because of you and your decisions?_
> _Perhaps you have a family at home that all survives and thrives because you bring home the bacon?_
> _Perhaps you're the one teaching a class or a workshop?_
> _Perhaps you're the one they put in charge at the church or the country club because you're the go-to boss man that gets things done?_

 **_Look, being the boss or being in charge doesn't mean you have all the answers_**.

It Just means that you're tasked with the responsibility of having the final say. Many people avoid being the boss for this very reason. They don't like having it all fall on their shoulders.

What if I'm wrong? What if I mess something up? What if I do that one thing they said never do? What if someone gets hurt?

What if—what if—what if...? It's endless.

Let's call it what it is:

A boss is a decision maker of some type and someone's who's in charge of something.

Doesn't matter if you're a girl or a boy, man or a woman, old or young, or anything in between any of those. It's just a title. A temporary moment in your life where something or somebody's depending on you and you're tasked with it. And, you may be the boss of people and also have bosses that you report to.

The first time someone becomes a boss it's often scary.

All those **"what if"** questions pop in and try to steal your thunder. If it goes well, though, or if that person's shielded heavily, oftentimes that person starts craving the feeling that comes with being in charge and having power. Some might say they become **power hungry.**

Those that have never really been in charge of anything in their lives are dangerous in these roles—because they don't understand the ramifications of their decisions.

If they're not used to making large-scale decisions that affect others, everyone will be in for a rocky road. *These new bosses don't know what information to trust nor who to get it from.*

A lot of small business owners struggle with this because they just wanted to have their own business so they didn't have to work for someone else. Then, as business started growing, they had to hire folks who now depend on them to do all those things. It's not easy without a solid infrastructure and background in management or decision making or planning and a lot of business owners get over-whelmed quickly, especially if they're a part of running the day-to-day operations.

Here's some everyday questions that bosses might face:

> *Is this a good price?*
> *Is it the best price I can get?*
> *Is it the highest quality?*
> *What are the options?*
> *What will our customers think?*
> *How quickly can it get here?*
> *Should our prices be higher or lower?*
> *What are others doing?*
> *Should I pay more to have it shipped quicker?*
> *Who's waiting on this?*
> *What can they do in the meantime?*
> *What happens when someone calls in sick?*
> *Who covers the shift?*
> *What should I be doing for returning customers?*
> *Who's closing the shop tonight?*
> *What insurance policy do we have that covers problems like this?*

Being a boss doesn't mean you know it all—
But it means you have to decide.

And yes, decision making is a skill and the more you do it the easier it becomes. Having a framework for decisions is good in many cases, but so is intuition and the right information. Part of how you get there is who you have on your team as resources. You know, people that supply you with the right information or, in the absence of people, a website or support group that has similar people to you that struggle with the same thing. Or, perhaps you have friends, advisors or consultants you meet up with to go over these kinds of things.

Just make sure the information is from dependable sources and that it's readily available as many decisions, if not made quickly, can backfire.

So yeah, while the buck stops here, it's often met with someone who's had a lot of experience in that kind of thing, whatever it is. Else, the buck truly does stop there and has to wait for the boss to make a decision after he or she gets enough information to act on.

If you're tasked with being the boss, don't just abuse that power and boss people around. No one deserves bosses like that. Use it as a stepping stone towards leading people. A boss, by definition, means someone who's in charge, but that also gives you the power to make a difference. It's a chance to actually lead those around you and build them up. An opportunity to provide your team (whoever that comprises of) with the right tools, the right information and the right guidance so that they, in turn, provide the same to you when you need it.

So, if you're the boss, make it mean something other than a title.

Being the boss—and acting like a child—is anything but a boss move.

SECRET #10

Being the boss is not about having all the answers but about shouldering the responsibility of making decisions. This chapter reveals that effective leadership requires a blend of experience, knowledge, and a willingness to seek advice, emphasizing that the power to lead is an opportunity to make a positive difference by empowering and guiding those around you.

11

STRONG VS. WEAK LEADERS

Strong leaders don't just create followers—
They create more leaders.

Strong leaders look to hire—*or be surrounded by*—smart people, and they help those folks develop into better versions of themselves. True leaders lead by example and give those around them the time, support, and feedback they need to improve in ways that wouldn't have been possible otherwise.

Weak leaders create weak followers—and often surround themselves with **yes men** (it says *"men"* but it's both men and women).

Yes men are always there—*smiling and agreeing with those who have authority over them*—in order to gain favor. *Yes men* avoid conflict and always seem to be on board with what the authority figure states.

Strong leaders are secure in themselves—and welcome feedback.

These leaders take in clues, information, training, education, and criticism—all in the attempt to improve themselves and their offerings to those that surround them.

Weak leaders are insecure and often reject feedback.

These leaders believe they know it all, are not open to change, don't take suggestions, often run over those that work with them, and think that being a leader means bossing *yes men* around.

Once you spot a *yes man,* follow them around—and you'll see just how many so-called leaders they've attached themselves to. You'll see very quickly how many weak leaders you have in your community.

> ***Once you spot an actual leader, watch carefully who they surround themselves with—and you'll find all those in your community that are truly making a difference.***

Yes men have a tendency to do more damage than all the others as they encourage and support the ideas and beliefs of authority figures, seemingly giving them more and more power, without adding any real value. *Yes men* are found on boards of directors, in middle management, on front lines, in churches, throughout our government, at town hall meetings, in major corporations, throughout our medical profession, and in schools.

It's cult-like—and sickening to watch from afar.

Worse is that so many yes men don't even realize they're doing it.
They think it's the right thing to do—because they're surrounded by others that are doing the same thing. They're just so used to agreeing with authority figures that they think nothing of it—and then teach their children to simply comply with those who have authority.
(I'm not talking about police here).

> *We need more leaders who create leaders.*
> *We need more people who are willing to stand up for what's right—and have conversations.*
> *We need people who take in reams of information and make sense of it for the masses.*

We need people who are willing to look at the true impact of their decisions on humanity and not just on the bottom line.
We need more people wiling to make those around them better, faster, stronger and smarter so we can all be better off.
We need more people who are wiling to say no instead of yes.

If you want to have a true impact on others—get out there and lead from the heart.

Start small and build something great. Leaders will show up all around you and you'll all be better off tomorrow than today.

You'll find people who are true to their word—those that are serious about making things better, those that bring solid ideas to the table, and those that are honest about whatever's up for debate. You'll also find some with backbones—that are willing to stand up for what's right in the face of opposition.

That's where strong leaders are made, at the heart of serving others.

And, for the record, I just can't see why anyone would willingly choose to be a *yes man*—or, worse, be a leader who surrounds themselves with a whole group of them.

SECRET #11

True leadership is about empowering others to become leaders themselves, fostering growth, and embracing feedback. This chapter exposes the damaging nature of "yes men," who, by unquestioningly supporting authority figures, contribute to a cult-like environment and hinder genuine progress, emphasizing the need for leaders who prioritize meaningful impact and encourage open dialogue.

12

PERSPECTIVE

'm not like you.
And you're not like them.
They're not like me.
We're all not like each other.

I'm me, you're you, they're themselves—
And so are those folks over there... on the other side of the fence.

We're all just out here doing whatever it is we do best—
And trying to get through.

For some of us, everything seems to be going just right.
For others, we can't catch a break.

Are you the best version of yourself?
Nope. None of us are.

You might be enough though, just the way you are.

Or, perhaps you want to improve and build on something you've been working on?

You're probably way ahead of many others who think they've got it all together.

Perspective is funny like that.

Living in the digital world is rough.

Not only do we have access to more information than ever, we have a skewed view of the world based on what the algorithms let us see...
and that's not helping.

Until we can be okay with our differences—*and celebrate them*—we stay stagnant.

If we're afraid to have conversations with others who aren't like us, we can't get better at this human experience.

So, keep doing what you're doing—and learn about others:

> *Ask questions.*
> *Get to know them or their business.*
> *Find out about their beliefs.*
> *Go deeper than you did yesterday.*
> *Engage in a way that contributes.*

Just don't keep to yourself.

And if you're truly a leader, listen to this next part carefully:

Today, there's someone who needs to hear from you:

> *Someone needs the expertise that only you have.*
> *Someone needs the help that only you can provide.*
> *Someone needs your perspective because it's different than theirs.*
> *Someone needs to know that you care about them as a person.*
> *Someone needs you to be the authentic you and show them the way.*

And, *you* just might be that someone to someone else.

Though we're all different, have different backgrounds, have vastly different experiences in this world, and see things from our own perspectives—we all have to co-exist and find ways to help each other, work together and thrive in our own communities.

Turns out, when we look at it from *THAT* perspective—
I am just like you after all.

SECRET #12

Embracing and celebrating our differences while engaging with others is essential for personal and collective growth. By recognizing our unique perspectives and reaching out to contribute, we can break down barriers, foster connections, and discover common ground, ultimately realizing that, in the broader context of the human experience, we share more similarities than differences.

13

HOW DO YOU KNOW?

How do you know?

How do you know there's a race problem?
How do you know that cases of some new disease are as high as they say?
How do you know we're experiencing terrible drought conditions and that we'll all soon be out of food?
How do you know there are aliens in the skies?
How do you know the economy's never been better than what it currently is?
How do you know the earth is round?
How do you know that what they're spraying in the skies is actually designed to help us?
How do you know our water's safe to drink?
How do you know all the new cell towers are safe for humans?
How do you know what countries we're supposed to feel bad for right now?
How do you know how to feel, in general?

No, I mean that, ***how do you ACTUALLY know?***

Friends, we don't really **KNOW** any of what I just asked—we're all just led to believe that we do.

And, when we're questioned on who it is we're listening to, we defend our sources as though we know—
but we don't.

Whatever it is **YOU** want to believe, it's out there.
Whatever it is **THEY** want us to believe—believe me, it's out there too and being broadcast 24/7.

I mean, usually it's either TV, internet, radio, or written, right?
Well... what if those major **channels** get controlled?

As leaders, it's important to not follow others blindly.

Narratives are easy to play out in your head once you see what all's being spewed. Red, blue, black, white—*it doesn't matter*—it's being made for you to believe and yes, it's believable.

Not sure what happened to the old **"trust, but verify"** mantra, but it seems to have gone away and we need to bring it back.

You can even verify lies by finding other sources that didn't verify them that'll stand up and say they're true.

Think: *fact-checkers.*

And, you can find videos and stories that contradict true stories just as quickly. Ugh.

> *It's all part of the psychological warfare that we're a part of right now. Nothing is to be believed and yet we're supposed to believe something.*

So, yeah, how do you know?
You don't. Neither do I.

I have ideas and stories and beliefs about how and why it's all coming together based on thousands of inputs—but I don't actually **KNOW.**
I rely on people too.

Good people are being misled, smart people are falling into traps, and so are people that are against it all.

Common sense is to be trusted now more than ever—but on what?

> *Deep fake videos,*
> *Video editing,*
> *Holograms,*
> *Stories that are made up,*
> *Definitions that are being rewritten,*
> *Fake news stories that are being shown over and over and over.*

What's real and what's not?

There's no good answer here—other than to not believe any of what's being broadcast for the masses.

If I were you...

> *I wouldn't believe the hype—as the sources are unverifiable.*
> *I wouldn't make decisions for your business or family if it's*
> *swayed by what the news is telling you to do.*
> *I wouldn't do anything that people recommend if there are parties*
> *or organizations that are being incentivized.*
> *I wouldn't trust people, organizations or industries that say we*
> *should blindly trust them without questioning anything.*
> *And I certainly wouldn't watch any of the mainst.... news stations to*
> *get a "feel" for anything going on.*

Unless, of course...
you know how you know.

SECRET #13

The truth lies in the acknowledgment that in today's information landscape, certainty is elusive, and narratives are often manipulated. This chapter urges skepticism, emphasizing the importance of not blindly trusting information, questioning sources, and recognizing the complexities of a world where discerning truth requires a nuanced approach beyond what mainstream channels might present.

14

LIFE'S KAYAK

Y ou are it.

You're the one that can make it happen.
Not me. Not them. Not some stranger. Not us. *You.*

A team of one.

Sometimes, we're all we've got.

We have to find our way.
We have to re-balance.
We have to breathe whatever's in the air.
We have to paddle when we no longer want to.
We have to change course.
We have to fight the elements.

Or... we just... drift off.

Today, more than ever, our lives resemble being on a kayak.
We can work together or be on teams or even be on the same lake,
but we have to be accountable to ourselves first.

Take care of ourselves, then we can help others.

If you're struggling with your own kayak—you're dead in the water.
So might be those who depend on you.

As a leader, it's important to believe in yourself AND your ability to help others.

We all need each other—but we have to be taking care of some of these things on our own as well.

Saddle up, paddle up, and set your course.

SECRET #14

The concealed wisdom here is a reminder that in the vast sea of life, YOU are the captain of your own vessel. It emphasizes the importance of self-reliance, personal accountability, and the need to navigate one's own path before extending a helping hand to others, encapsulating the essence of taking charge of your life's journey.

15

THE GOODS

It doesn't take long at all.

If you want to be critical of someone and find their faults, it's easy. And, the more subjective you are, the easier it becomes. Use words like:

"I feel like you don't...,"
"I think maybe you should...,"
"I have a feeling you...,"
"I don't like how you...,"
"I get uneasy when you...,"
Or even something like, *"I can't stand it when..."*

Or, if you really need to be able to find fault and hold them to it, create metrics—*for anything and everything*—and then objectively measure it all.

Like, maybe, you have to clock in and clock out within two minutes of your shift starting and ending. Or, that you have to take exactly fifteen minute breaks every two hours—no more, no less. You can't take more than ten seconds in between phone calls. You're allowed only one restroom break per shift and no more than ten minutes.

You could set things up like that all day long and find thousands of ways to catch your employees doing something wrong. This way you're always the enforcer and they're always afraid. Some people love this kind of power and they abuse it. The more you know about someone, the easier it is to hold it over them—especially when it comes to promotions, raises, bonuses, and awards.

But you know what's hard?

Getting the 'goods' on your employees—finding ways of catching them **in the wild** doing something worth praising. It's hard because it's not the norm for most leaders. It goes against what most think **management** should be doing. It's counterintuitive when it comes to what most think **leading** is about.

 So, let's explore how this mindset could work for you.

First, you have to care enough about your employees to implement something like this. Because, if you do, it's infinitely easier than if you don't. If you care, it'll be like putting on a pair of glasses that allow you to see things from the perspective you need. Not rose-colored glasses, per se—but definitely a lens that'll pinpoint and magnify actions you won't see otherwise.

Second, you need a place to capture what you see, what you find, and what you hear. Could be a personnel file, a document set up for that employee, a notepad with their name on it, or whatever works best for you.

Third, you have to be creative and use the information you gather in a positive way. Don't just collect it and let it sit, use it to pump your team members up, to build confidence, and to help others see what's possible. It's also great to have when you want to thank your team members publicly, to reinforce positivity, or merely to let them know that they're making a difference.

What does it look like?

That'll be something different for every company, and every position, but here are some starting points of things to start thinking about. And, when I say **"they,"** or **"them,"** it's your team members—each and every one of them.

> *Start with looking for what they do well or what they do great. You know, their strengths. What they've improved on. What you like about how they do a certain something.*

Ask customers about them (privately). Like, after they've worked with someone. Capture the quotes and who said it... and why. Ask specific questions that lead customers towards the positive.

Ask co-workers what they like about working with them. Not in front of anyone, but casually. Again, be intentional, but aim it towards the positive.

Keep track of trends.
Perhaps someone is always early and helps set something up. Or, they always help their teammates finish their work before they leave. Maybe they take initiative to start new things without anyone asking them. Or, that they're always positive and people like to be around them. Or, that you love their creativity and how they always contribute in meaningful ways that positively affect the team.

And there's something else.
You can ask and find out about other things they do outside of work, and praise that. Maybe they have a YouTube channel you could talk about. Maybe they do community service and help the homeless on weekends. Maybe they sing at church or coach a little league team. Maybe they have a major milestone coming up like an anniversary or birthday.

You can find the "goods" on someone if you look, I promise.

If your goal is to celebrate those around you and make them feel good about being there, then that's what you do. It takes work, but it's worth it. It takes time, but it'll pay off.

That said, there are plenty of things you can celebrate if you piece it together right. Think about the following as starting points:

> *Acts of kindness,*
> *Work ethic,*
> *Stepping up as a leader,*
> *Passion,*
> *Inclusiveness,*
> *Overcoming obstacles,*
> *Learning from mistakes,*
> *Dedication,*
> *Perseverance,*
> *Overall positivity,*
> *Going the extra mile, or*
> *Being customer-focused.*

The only way you get there is by leading with intent.
Truly caring about others and highlighting *them.* And this can work with any group of people you're leading. It could be in a small business, in corporate America, at a church, in a classroom, on a football field, or at home with your kids.

Oh, and by the way, very few leaders do this.

People need to hear that they matter.
They need to know that someone notices when they do something good. They need a proverbial pat on the back that says, *"I see you."*

 ***And heck, if you're in a position where you can turn the "goods" into actual goods, by all means, push for tangible reinforcement.***

Goods are made **GREAT** when they result in monetary bonuses, salary raises, or additional paid time off. If you can make it happen, do so. It might also be things like health and and wellness reimbursements because of them, a gift of company swag, professional development opportunities, or even a paid lunch for the team in their honor.

As a leader, it's important we ***"manage"*** our teams, but that means we also have opportunities. If you can find ways to pick people apart, you can certainly find ways to build them up. It just takes a leader who cares. And when you do, you'll be that much closer to being a leader worth following.

So, go out there and get the goods on your people—
They need it... and so do you!

SECRET #15

The secret to effective leadership lies in shifting the focus from fault-finding to recognizing and celebrating the positive attributes of team members. By intentionally seeking out and documenting the strengths, achievements, and positive behaviors of employees, leaders create a culture of appreciation and empowerment. Taking the time to acknowledge and reward the "goods" not only boosts team morale but also fosters a work environment where individuals feel valued, ultimately contributing to the leader's success and the overall success of the team.

16

MEH

My daughter looked at me and said,
"I don't know if she understood, Dad."

I pondered this for only a few seconds before answering—and then my answer was clear. But, first, my perspective needs to talk...

Businesses are not cold, lifeless buildings that simply hoard products we consume and pay dearly for—just to come back to do it again and again with an automated checkout procedure.

Or, at least they shouldn't be.

Granted, that's the direction some people would like to see this world go in. This way, we eliminate all the useless humans that ramble on and on and suck up resources—when we could replace them with computer systems that we just have to invest in and program once (with a million updates).

Right?
So, here's the deal.

I learned long ago—*when I was 17*—how important it was to personally greet people or acknowledge them in some fashion within seconds of entering a room.

I wasn't just unaware of this prior, I was **BLATANTLY** unaware.

The girl I was dating at the time was with me, and we were practicing for a dance performance. Her parents came to watch, and I noticed them walk in—and then I gave them something to actually... watch.

Allegedly, I didn't acknowledge them in any form or fashion *(not even a smile or a head nod or a wave)*—nor personally greet them. I just went about my way and thought everything was great.

Then, later that night, I got blasted with an earful as to how disrespectful I was—how pissed off they were that I didn't make *any attempt* to say hello, and how rude of a person I was.

Mind you, I didn't do anything. Literally.

But, in that very moment, I understood. I listened carefully to what their complaint was, and it hit me like a brick.

I thought, wow—I could easily have remedied this had I even pretended to care. By doing nothing, I let their imagination run wild into thinking they weren't important and that they didn't matter—and, whether true or not, it doesn't age the way wine does.

I made it a point from the next day forward to be better—

> *To say hello to people.*
> *To acknowledge their existence.*
> *To greet them in a way that makes them feel important.*
> *To use names when I can (I often cheat and use name tags if I'm in a store).*

It mattered then. It matters now.

Heck, I'd say it matters now more than ever—as we're all facing the possibility of being replaced by self-checkouts, online interactions, remote overseas customer support, and driverless delivery trucks and whatnot.

So, to my point—
When someone walks in on something I'm a part of, I make it a point to include them. When I walk into something else, I make it a point to make sure I'm included.

Now, I understand that while this particular girl might have dated a lot of people, the vast majority of folks I know never learned this lesson from her parents. If you had been in my shoes though—and heard what I heard, and saw what I saw, and dealt with what I dealt with—you'd be making darned sure you don't neglect anyone because, frankly, if you know, you know.

You know?

Now, I'll be Jen and circle back. My daughter and I walked into a local coffee shop. We saw that there were two young ladies working. One was making coffee and the other was looking at her phone. The one that was looking at her phone looked up and made eye contact with us as we opened the door—and then went right back to her phone.

No acknowledgment. No greeting. No "Welcome to Moe's!"
No welcome whatsoever.

The *"Welcome to Moe's!"* would have been cool though—and I'd have been impressed... but puzzled.

After about a minute, she walks over to the cash register where we were standing, picks up her order pad, looks up with a straight, emotionless face and says, *"What do you want?"*

Me, being me, said, *"Hi, good morning,"* and then just smiled and waited for a response. A moment of silence, if you will.

She responded with, *"Do you know what you want?"* I actually did know what I wanted, so I restated it in a way she would understand...

"Hi, good morning."

I wanted to hear her say, *"Good morning."* I wanted some kind of a *"Welcome to our store!"* I wanted to feel some level of appreciation for walking in to this particular coffee shop when I had several other choices. I wanted to believe that I mattered to her.

What I got as my *first impression* was essentially a coffee mug with three large letters spelling out **MEH.**

Interestingly, by her inaction and personal phone usage when we walked in, I could tell she wasn't busy. She didn't have crowds of people lining up at the door. She didn't seem interested in being there, whatsoever. And, she looked bothered by the small talk.

She stared at me. I stared at her. Her eyes cut over to my daughter—and then back to me.

She then said, *"Do you need more time?"*

"Hi, good morning—yes, I'd like a large cup of black coffee please."

She responded with, *"We don't have drip coffee here. Is a Caffe' Americano okay?"*

My bewilderment became more apparent than ever and, needless to say, that drink is what I walked out with several minutes later.

A coffee shop with no black coffee? *(enter dumb look on my face here with me nodding) * True story*

I let myself out with my own parting line of, *"Hope you have a great Monday!"* to which there was a brief smile and a response of, *"Come back and see us."*

So, here's the thing—
She looked to be a college student. So did the other girl. At some point she had been trained by someone who presumably owns the place (it wasn't a franchise). The owner may or may not have made it a point to cover this little detail—I'll never know.

She did know to use the words *"Come back and see us"* though, which equates to *"Please bring us more money."*

Note who this favors (it's not me).

But, what I do know is that her current behavior and lack of people skills is what will get us all replaced in the future.

I'm not saying we should all date the girl I dated when I was 17—but we all need someone to let us know the importance of appreciating others just for showing up.

I never did get the *"Good morning!"* I was hoping for, but I did get to explain it to my daughter—who now understands the importance.

I'm not better than anyone—
But I won't be ignored nor feel like I don't matter.

If I have to be the welcoming party in someone else's store—you can bet I will. And, based on my reception, I have no problem letting myself out as well.

I get to choose where I shop, how I spend my money, and what I form habits doing—based on how I'm treated and how I feel as a customer who doesn't have to be there.

And so do you.

For leaders, everywhere—*especially those in the service industry (heck, we're ALL in that in some form or fashion)*—know that *first impressions* matter.

And there's a BIG difference in "MEH" and "Good morning!"

SECRET #16

The covert wisdom whispers that in the realm of business and life, the currency of personal acknowledgment holds more value than any transaction. This chapter unveils the silent power of a warm greeting, a genuine smile, and the ability to make someone feel appreciated—a timeless principle in a world that sometimes seems enamored with automation and cold efficiency.

17

THE RIGHT WAY?

There's no right way to do the wrong thing.

There may be ways to get away with it,
but that doesn't make it right.

And, we've all been there.

Perhaps it was taking something inadvertently, or speeding when we didn't realize it, or telling a white lie to protect someone's feelings, or taking more than our fair share of something just so someone else couldn't?

Maybe it was using a cell phone while driving, or jaywalking, or littering, or turning right on a red light, or rolling through a stop sign when no one was looking?

It doesn't make anyone a bad person—it just simply says we're human, we all make mistakes, and we sometimes get away with them.

The key word there is mistake.

Other 'wrong' things in this world are intentionally done where
the wrongdoers still get away with it.

Some good examples here include:

The creation of different types of bioengineered foods (plants/ animals, etc),

Medicines that are designed to get you hooked and unable to get free,

Companies that create protocols that prohibit employees from speaking freely,

Programs that fund the spraying of chemicals into our atmosphere that affect all of us,

Towers that emit extremely high levels of radiation in the middle of neighborhoods,

Tech aimed at eliminating the need for humans in the future, and

Products that contain carcinogenic chemicals known to damage cells and harm our health.

Legal? Sure.
Wrong? I suppose you get to decide.

And, that's interesting too—as some people will argue that it's legal, therefore okay. I'm not *"some people."* I'd like to counter that with: *"Who made the laws?"* and *"Who lobbied for this to be legal?"*

Oftentimes, the companies hide behind their corporate shield and hire legal teams that spend their days crafting both policy and *'terms of use'* nonsense that protects them while putting pure garbage out into the world at our expense.

We—the collective WE—continue to allow the degradation of our own society by supporting these things over and over.

Not just by allowing them, but by:

Buying the products,
Sharing stories about the products,
Not reading labels,

Not reading fine print,
Not reading terms and conditions,
Not showing up at community gatherings where these things are
*   talked about and voted on,*
Supporting certain platforms that remove free speech, and
Not standing up or out against any of it once we find out.

Every. Single. Day.

I'm learning more and more of **what all we've been lied to about—**
(schools, media, online "trusted" sources, etc.)

> *Just because a company buries the fine print thirty pages deep*
> *   and they say, "well, we put it out there," **doesn't make it right.***
> *Just because a company says they're allowed to do something*
> *   because of some cockamamie bill that passed in the middle of the*
> *   night with 9,000 other little things around it where no one could*
> *   see or find it, **doesn't make it right.***

Intuitively, we all know right from wrong. Making mistakes is one thing and on the ground level. Misleading people and doing this crap intentionally is on a whole different level that's much higher than most people want to reach for.

Or, is it lower?

When I say we all need to help each other, do know that it's much bigger than just some *thing* we've all been duped about over the last several years...

> *It's wide.*
> *It's deep.*
> *It's well-funded.*
> *And it's all-encompassing.*

Once you see it, you can't unsee it.

Right is right. Wrong is wrong.

As leaders, it's up to us to make sure we do what's right for the long-term benefit of society.

Say it with me:

There's no right way to do the wrong thing.

And let's move forward by speaking up, sharing information, and making changes in our personal lives.

Again, *there's no right way to do the wrong thing!*

SECRET #17

The uncomfortable truth here is that while there may be ways to cloak the wrong, there's inherent wisdom in recognizing that legality doesn't equate to morality. It beckons us to scrutinize the intentional actions masked under legal veils, urging us to discern right from wrong and foster a collective consciousness that transcends the deceptive allure of legality.

18

WINNING

Teams can win without winning and lose without losing.

"How's that?" you say. It's easy. Winning is different from losing.

Winning is about being better—better than you were last week, better than you were yesterday, and better tomorrow because of what you do today.

Winning is also about showing up, working together and overcoming obstacles.

Winning is doing more of the right things, at the right time, in the right place, than your competitors. Winning is creating a culture that people want to belong to. Winning teams build each other up and create leaders. Winning teams look out and care for each other.

Losing is consistently being mediocre.

Nothing changes from day to day and the team never really gets better. Often, losing is—*by any measurable standard*—a result of being the worse of two teams. *Losing teams lack care.*

Losing regularly has a bunch of individuals playing for themselves. Losing is blaming and claiming bad luck, weather, field constraints, or refs are the reasons for failure. *Losing teams tear each other down.*

Winning is a mindset—but, sadly, so is losing.

Turns out, teams can—*and often do*—get a **W** in their Win column just by being present when another team beats itself.

In other words, **"they didn't win, the other team lost."**

A winning team is different than a team winning. A winning attitude is present and found at the top of the organization and throughout the coaching staff—and it touches each and every team member.

Winning is contagious—*and the team spirit spreads into the community.* Not surprisingly, people truly enjoy watching and supporting winning teams, even when they lose. *Winning teams are likable—if not charismatic-like.*

Interestingly, "winning teams" are not just found in sports.
Many organizations have winning teams, just like many of them have losing teams.

Small businesses that are winning help build community. People want to support them and, rarely, is it just based on their prices. The attitudes of employees, management's involvement, the handling of problems, the attention to details, and the willingness to make customers feel like they matter are all keys to winning.

We all, secretly, want to be a part of winning teams—sports, organizations, churches, school boards, committees.

The thing is, we all have to step up and let others know what's working, what's not, and what we can do to make things better.

 *You don't have to have a title to be a leader and make a difference—just a voice.*

If you're going to belong to a team, do your part to make it a winning team. You don't have to **win** all the time in order to make an impact and make the world around you a much more enjoyable place.

For those who've been a part of an actual winning team, you know what I'm talking about. Stand up and shout it from the rooftops. It's worth being involved. Maybe some athletic director somewhere needs to see this. Or a coach. Or a player. Someone needs to know it's okay to not focus on wins and losses—*but rather, on impact*—and what better way than by creating a winning environment.

As a leader, it's important you get out there and WIN—
But it's not important you beat the other team.

SECRET #18

Winning transcends mere victory; it's an ethos, an attitude, and a collective effort to be better every day. Whether in sports, organizations, or life, it's about building a winning culture, uplifting others, and making an impact beyond the scoreboard.

19

PURPOSE OR PASSION?

Which one's more important: *PURPOSE or PASSION?*
Over the years I've heard many arguments for both.

To simplify, passion is about emotions and it's the *"do what you love"* side of things.

Purpose is the *"why you're doing what you're doing"* side of things.

Passion is inwardly focused. | Purpose is outwardly focused.

Passion is about emotions. | Purpose is about the reasons.

Are they both important? Yes.
Can you be successful with one or the other, but not both? Yes.
Can you be successful without passion or purpose? Sadly, yes.
Can you have both at all times? Emphatically, **YES!**

I like the old saying:

> **"Passion is what gets you started and Purpose is what keeps you going."**

It certainly can be that way, and often is—but it doesn't have to be.

It seems a lot of people spend their lives looking to find that *ONE* thing that fills them with passion.

Many never find it.

It's kind of like happiness—
The harder you look externally, the less likely you are to find it.

I've used many conversations over the years with my kids to help them understand this next part. Hopefully, if I describe it well enough, it'll make sense in a single paragraph that goes like this:

If you develop a passion for helping or serving, in general, and then couple it with learning life skills with the purpose of contributing to society in a positive way, you'll never feel unfulfilled.

In other words, bring your passion with you into whatever job, task, chore, assignment, or project you're doing.

You can be passionate about being thorough, or being clean, or doing a job well.

Not obsessive, but passionate.

Then, no matter what you get involved in, you end up with a smile on your face and those around you genuinely enjoy your company.

Doing this, you'll often hear things like:

> *"You look like you really enjoy your job!"*

Truth is, *you will,* because you enjoy the *"doing"* portion and it doesn't really matter what ***it*** is.

You're not enjoying ***it*** because you're getting paid to. That's different.

Now, don't get me wrong—you also have to consider what kind of money you **want** to have or **need** to have as you're deciding.

Growing up in the 80's and early 90's, I dreamed of being a park ranger, but I abandoned those dreams when I looked at the commitment and pay.

It just wasn't for me and it didn't align with the type of life I wanted. I explored many other industries and expanded my dreams.

> *Once you develop a work ethic that combines both passion and purpose, you can take it with you and do anything you want— and still be fulfilled. It opens the door to possibility.*

When you get to this point, everything excites you and you feel like the world's playground is just waiting to be enjoyed.

And, you get to choose who you jump in and play with.

Now, if you chase money instead, you end up more likely to compromise your belief in passions and/or purpose and tell yourself it's just what you **HAVE** to do.

It's a slippery slope as you'll find that there's never enough money and there will always be someone with "more" than you have.

Worse yet, is when you end up using money as an indicator of success. Watch out for people or companies (or politicians) that have this mindset.

Success should never have a dollar sign or figure associated. It's a mindset. Like happiness, it's not tangible.

It's about accomplishments—
And doing what's right because it's what's right.

Passion and purpose are both important—but they're not easily measured. Think character. Think integrity. *None can be measured on paper. All are essential.*

As a leader, if you can develop both passion and purpose for everything you do—and then bring them with you—you're going to change the world.

And, as a side benefit, every **moment** or **job** or **task** becomes one you can enjoy and then look back on and smile.

Even the ones that end in some type of lesson that better prepares us for life going forward.

SECRET #19

The secret to a fulfilled life lies in merging passion and purpose, making every endeavor an enjoyable and meaningful experience. It's not about chasing money or external markers of success but fostering a mindset of integrity, character, and doing what's right, transcending the tangible and embracing the intangible aspects of a well-lived life.

20

PAIN POINTS

had no idea.

I couldn't understand why it was all so different. Why conversations didn't work. Why the responses were different. Why the business owners did what they did. Why the parents acted the way they did. Why there was no homework. Why people wouldn't let us help.

Was it me?

I had told this story umpteen times. Every time I told it I was looking for an answer. A reason. Something to go on. Some kind of an understanding that would make it make sense.

And then it happened.

Some fifteen months after I started looking—a random conversation at an elementary school dance.

A talk that would change everything.

A talk that would get me to look at and see the world I was in now— *differently.*

"You're WAY more perceptive than anyone I've ever met," she said.

A compliment, indeed, but one that left my head turned. She was smiling and she ended that statement with silence—silence that felt like forever.

And that made me feel like I was missing something.

"How much do you know about poverty?" she inquired.

Me, being me I smiled back and cringed.
 "A little?" I responded with my teeth clinched and eyes a bit squinted.

She nailed it.

This was the thing I was missing.
The missing link.
The broken chain.
The piece of the puzzle that I couldn't find.

 She recommended a book for me to go through called, *The Framework for Understanding Poverty.*

Over the course of the next seven days this very book would consume me. I chose the audiobook and listened to it three different times (it's only about seven hours if I'm not mistaken).

A week later she asked me if I'd had a chance to look into the book. She had one of those smirks on her face where you just know she's thinking the answer's no.

I then lit up and shared how my week had gone.
How my mind had been blown.

Turns out I knew hardly anything about it:

> *I didn't know the differences in generational poverty versus situational.*
>
> *I didn't have a clue about the stereotypes for poverty, middle class, and upper class.*
>
> *I didn't know how different the conversations at home are, how the entertainment was different nor how having access to information mattered.*
>
> *I didn't understand why the businesses were set up the way they were.*

I could see it all for the first time.

In a single week I'd gone through three of the four stages of competence in the learning quadrant relating to poverty.

The first stage is called **Unconscious Incompetence,** and it's when you *"don't know what you don't know"*—as in, I had no idea what I was getting into when speaking on the subject or what the book could be about.

The second stage, **Conscious Incompetence**, is when you realize how much there is to something—and that you don't know it at all. Like, you become aware of your own deficiencies. That happened as I listened to the audiobook the first time.

The third stage, **Conscious Competence**, is when you understand something or can do it, but it takes lots of thought. You get it, but it's not natural to you yet and you still have to work at it or think it through by reviewing notes or looking at steps or whatever. By the third time I'd listened to the audiobook, I was getting it. I'd taken notes and started really digging deep.

I thought back to all my conversations in our area and I understood where I went wrong. I could see how we didn't connect, and what I was missing. And I understood a little more about why so many in the community acted and interacted the way they did.

I also went all the way back to my childhood and saw how the people I was surrounded with (family, friends, mentors, etc.) were in each of the different classes. I saw how each had a distinct advantage over some things and wasn't interested in others, at all.

Since this happened I've probably had twenty or so conversations about the book, how powerful it was, and what it meant to me... but I doubt very seriously anyone else looked into it.

And that's because something has to matter to you. To me. To each of us. We have to have the proverbial bridge on fire before we're truly concerned. A real-life pain point. For me, it had happened. I was reaching out and trying to make sense of it because of how frustrated I was.

My point is this.

If you've struggled with connecting with people—*could be your team members, co-workers, people in your area, folks at church, etc.*—and are open to the idea that it may just be you and your inability to *meet them where they are,* please consider this book.

It's a good starting point.

You'll be glad you did and I guarantee you'll have a new appreciation for understanding people you may not have understood.

But the same holds true for other pain points as well.

For example, I've struggled to team up with what I perceive to be leaders who need help. Managers, small business owners, coaches, teachers, and those in community government. By leaning in and assessing my perceived pain point (their resistance to change or early rejection of my feedback or thoughts), I've been able to isolate potential variables that could be altered.

Turns out, there are things I could do differently that might result in better outcomes.

What I learned is that providing feedback or help to people who don't always ask for it is tricky.

How you present the feedback or thoughts matters.
The timing of when you offer anything up matters.
The order of the questions or thoughts, themselves, matters.
Getting their buy-in or permission matters.
Being specific, constructive, and framing things in a positive manner matters.
Respecting boundaries matters.
The words you use and how you use them matters.

Even with all of this, there are no guarantees—some people just don't want feedback or help, period. This is particularly difficult when it's something you just can't walk away from (think: small town, coaches, teachers, family-owned businesses, heck… families).

 **Can I change the past? No. Can I incorporate these ideas and concepts going forward? Absolutely.**

And that's the thing about life—at the very least, we get to live it.

For those who reflect, are open to something "better," and have a growth mindset, we get to live and learn.

Else, we just get into these repeated patterns that don't resolve themselves over time.

Your pain point might be something completely different.

And, for it to be a true pain point, you have to feel it. *Deeply.*
And have a deep-seated desire to remove it as a hurdle.

It could be:

> *Your weight,*
> *An addiction of some type,*
> *Small talk,*
> *Receiving compliments,*
> *Eating healthy, or*
> *Something as simple as making phone calls.*

Each of those examples could be a persistent problem you face and maybe the way you deal with it isn't working.

It takes someone coming to the realization that they struggle with something.

They have to acknowledge that what they've been doing might not bring the best results or just... hasn't worked.
Then they look for other ways that might work better.
Then they look to incorporate those things into their lives.

It's humbling.

Oh, and there's one other thing—you're being watched.
It might be your kids, grandkids, a co-worker, a customer, a neighbor, a friend, a boss, your team, or someone at church.
We all are.

But, in being watched it means that someone, somewhere, will notice:

> *When YOU take action.*
> *When you recognize the struggle and start searching.*
> *When you make positive changes.*
> *When you are open to the fact there may be a better way forward and do something about it.*
> *When you become a better version of yourself.*

Not only will they see you do it, *they'll be inspired* and they just might take their own actions.

And that's the kind of ripple leaders need to create.

We all get to choose, daily, how we want to show up.

Today, I'm showing up with new knowledge, skills, and thoughts about how to better lead others.

Tomorrow, I'll build off of today and see what I can glean.

Hope you do too.

SECRET #20

The secret to effective leadership lies in recognizing and addressing your blind spots. With an emphasis on self-awareness and understanding others on a deeper level, this chapter emphasizes bridging gaps and transformative realizations. The key lies in continuous self-reflection, learning, and the willingness to adapt leadership approaches to connect with and empower those around you.

21

IMPACT

I recently got into a discussion with a young man who talked about how *"successful"* a particular coach was and he shared that coach's lifetime record with me.

Having done quite a bit of coaching and training of coaches over the years, this is one of those topics that really revs my engines up... more than most.

I acknowledged the record and stated what I knew of the many people that absolutely hated playing for that particular coach.

He said, *"Yeah, but... he won a LOT of games."*

Again, I acknowledged the statement, but my thoughts were way ahead of him on the race track.

I smiled, shook my head in a somewhat disagreeing manner and said, *"Yeah... I guess I just don't see it the same way."*

"What do you mean? What else is there?" he said.
So I explained to him what I'm about to share with you.

Here goes...

Success at coaching has EVERYTHING to do with IMPACT.

No, not the impact of the coach.
The impact on the player—each and every player.
Impact that matters and changes people.
Impact that lasts a lifetime.

Now, for all of the middle school and high school coaches out there who just want to win, we need to talk—

> *If you think your job is to produce winning teams,*
> **you've already lost.**
> *If your athletic director looks at your wins and losses to determine*
> *your success,* **it's game over for you AND your team.**
> *If discipline is your thing and teaching kids compliance and how to*
> *obey orders is your goal,* **find a new hobby.**

Coaching isn't about winning—
Coaching is about developing people.

Doesn't matter if it's baseball, football, hockey, volleyball, golf, softball, lacrosse, tennis, cheerleading, track and field, swimming, archery, cross country, wrestling, or any other sport—everything hereafter applies and affects coaches, parents and players alike.

Coaching is a unique opportunity to shape and mold developing minds that are hungry.

At no point should coaches be given the job unless they understand how critical their role is.

> *It's not just another season.*
> *It's not just another team.*
> *It's not just another paycheck.*
> *It's not just another kid that shows up because they had nothing else*
> *to do.*

To be an impactful coach, one must accept full responsibility for his/her team.

An impactful coach would never just show up and wing it—
As preparing for a season takes discipline, structure and a working knowledge of:

> *Communication plans,*
> *Objective measurements,*
> *Goal-setting, and*
> *Skill-based teaching.*

All too often, coaches show up and pick teams based on the players who are the: showiest, loudest, tallest, fastest, strongest, biggest, or the ones who are children of friends or that come from high-profile parents.

No actual **criteria.**
No way to assess anything to be **fair.**
No real answers as to who they want on **their** team.

Right away this is a huge disadvantage for many kids who are ready, able and willing to play—but don't get the chance.

They just don't make the cut.

Now, some would say, *"That's life."*
And others say, *"Well you just weren't good enough."*

Usually, it's those who were picked without having to do anything other than just show up.

You see, a successful coach isn't just *someone who makes things fun.*

A successful coach isn't someone who just *yells a lot and is on some kind of a power trip as an authority figure.*

A successful coach isn't just someone who's solely *focused on winning.*

Successful coaches are a culmination of many **little things** that make a **BIG IMPACT** on players.

Here are my top twenty factors *(counting down, but in no particular order as they're ALL important)* that are mostly independent and strategies for what I consider...

 ### *The Road To SUCCESSFUL COACHING*

20. A successful *"head"* coach develops the mind of the players. The thoughts, the scenarios, the handling of mistakes, the changing of strategies, the evaluations of competition, the handling of winning, and the handling of losses. In addition, it's the day-to-day grind, the importance of *showing up* and accountability, the ins-and-outs of the game and how to handle adversity and manage teammates. A *"head"* coach helps players understand the mind game and all that goes with it.

19. A successful coach conveys his or her team vision in a way that inspires team members to set the bar higher and reach heights they never thought possible. This coach motivates the players on the daily and creates a culture and atmosphere of synergy while instilling values such as integrity, hard work, honesty, trust, commitment, humility, and respect.

18. A successful coach allows for mistakes. This coach doesn't lose control of emotions when mistakes are made, but rather keeps track of them to ensure mistakes are known to all team members and worked on as a part of practices. Mistakes often have consequences that need to be understood and put into the minds of players as to what happens, what the impacts are, and how to get out of them. Mistakes should be celebrated early and incorporated on a daily basis in order to minimize them as the season goes on.

17. A successful coach sets up measurable objectives and provides an environment for skill-based learning. Skills that are used in the sport, and essential for excelling. Skills that can be mastered independently and demonstrated. Skills that show progress over time, week after week, to show growth, regardless of wins and losses. Skills that can be captured on game film and recorded so everyone can see how well they're doing or where improvement is needed.

16. A successful coach assigns rotating leadership roles to team members and helps each member understand the power of effective leaders through words, actions and body language. This coach understands the importance of empowerment and he or she provides regular feedback regarding their roles and encourages them to become stronger and more confident in how they handle their teammates and situations.

15. A successful coach is consistent in decision making, strategy, attitude and coaching philosophy, but is always flexible enough to change and/or adjust based on new information when presented in a manner that warrants it. Consistency allows for all those around the coach to know what to expect and have a good basis for how and what is negotiable—and for when situations warrant further information or action.

14. A successful coach provides equal opportunity for all players on the team (this is more for middle school). Every player that shows up and puts the time in at practice should get equal playing time in games to see how well they perform. Growth happens quickly to those who get the opportunity. Unfortunately, so many great athletes quit playing sports in middle school as they realize how poorly organized it is and how the focus is on winning and not on the players.

13. A successful coach provides the players with constructive feedback on a daily basis and gives them tools to improve *AND* ways to measure it. After every game or match or event, every player should be required to reflect on their own performance accurately, ask questions and evaluate their team's performance in the same manner. This allows them to think, critically, about what they did right, what they need to improve on, what others did right and areas where the team needs improvement as a whole.

12. A successful coach is both competent (knowledge about the sport) and confident (self-assured) and is a leader that's worth following. This coach knows how to lead (not just be a boss) and can be trusted by any and all stakeholders to guide, teach and mentor their team.

11. A successful coach celebrates successes and effort of all the players. This coach looks for ways to celebrate actual achievements outside of wins and losses. Predetermined success measures that can be quantified. Effort that can be talked about and praised. In addition, this coach actively demonstrates good sportsmanship by celebrating successes of opposing teams and coaches as well.

10. A successful coach knows how to win *AND* can clearly communicate the process of winning. This coach understands defeat and knows how to channel it into motivation and lessons for growth. This coach is focused on the *"why"* of outcomes, rather than just results and drives change. Why did we win (full analysis)? Why did we lose (full analysis)? What changes do we make and why?

9. A successful coach sets up real-life or game-time scenarios regularly and practices with intent. This coach understands the importance of full immersion in practices in order to prepare their team for as many circumstances as possible. This coach does not just go through the motions of mind-numbing exercises, but rather, makes sure that every moment of practice is engaging, thought-provoking and helpful towards the goal of the entire team. Some call this **performance practice,** some call it **professional practice,** and some just call it, **practice.** If part of a team is on the bench, they have something to be watching and keeping track off at all times so they can help their teammates. If drills include running and the sport has a ball, this coach always ensures the ball is incorporated.

8. A successful coach communicates regularly with parents and allows for involvement. This coach is upfront and clear about what the expectations of the players are, what the goals of the team are, what's being worked on and why, and what is expected of parents. This coach also ensures that the parents have reasonable expectations of what the practices will be like, allows for open practices, what the involvement of parents should be at home, what the parents can do to help, what is reasonable behavior and what is not accepted.

7. A successful coach makes the players the priority and is all about building self-esteem through team-building and personal awareness protocols. This coach makes time to speak with each player, individually, and understand their goals, struggles, feelings, etc. This coach makes sure each player understands the importance of teamwork, the importance of treating others with respect, and the importance of representing your team in a positive manner both on and off the playing surface.

6. A successful coach conveys both honesty and integrity on and off the playing field. This coach does not waver or compromise on right versus wrong and knows that the right call is always objective and not just when it benefits him or her. This coach is always willing to fight for what's right even if it's at their own personal expense or the team's expense. This coach understands that rules, honesty and integrity are always in play.

5. A successful coach makes both talking and listening a priority. This coach helps players articulate questions and answers respectfully. Knowing how to pose questions, what to say, and how to do so in a manner that gets results rather than complaining or whining is important and an asset to a team. Teaching players to be active listeners is equally as important as it creates a culture of engaged teammates who have an interest in improvement.

4. A successful coach keeps track of all the little things and posts them publicly for the team and the parents. This allows for the players to have constant reinforcement of what they're doing right and build confidence in themselves as they go. This also helps when it comes to internal competitiveness of players, as the public statistics become a part of every player's daily check-in.

3. A successful coach talks about the importance of active warm ups using sport-specific drills that ramp up as blood starts flowing. This coach ensures players are set up with knowledge and understand how and when to stretch, how to minimize injury by using best-practices *AND* the importance of nutrition and hydration—as well as cool downs and taking care of your body outside of practices and games.

2. A successful coach demonstrates time management mastery and provides outlines and agendas for all practices. This coach is respectful to players and parents alike and starts each practice on time and ends at the exact time it was stated. Every player is aware of the impact and disruption caused by being late and parents know exactly how to schedule time based on the precedent set by the coach. Expectations are clear and met each and every day by all parties as mutual respect for time flows in all directions.

1. A successful coach sets up a feedback loop from both the players and the parents. This coach knows the importance of allowing for feedback **in a constructive manner** from everyone he or she is there to serve. The feedback loop here gives all players and parents the opportunity to voice concerns, give praise, ask questions, say what went right, share what they'd like to see more of, and offer any other thoughts that would be *helpful* to the coach or the team. Coaches should welcome this kind of input and encourage honesty to help them learn and grow as a coach. It helps complete the circle so that everybody gets better in the end.

You see, impact on players is lost when it comes to just winning and losing. Life lessons are easily taught in environments where the coach is truly in touch with putting players first—all players, not just the best. If you want to build a team of winners in the future, start with building a team who loves to learn. Learning about themselves, about their sport, about their teammates, about their skills, about their roles, about best practices, about their performances, about objective measurements, and about their community.

Every bit of what I just covered can be done in a fun environment and is lost if the coach is rude, demanding, uninterested or unprofessional at any point along the way. Boundaries need to be set, but within them can be an environment that absolutely lights a fire under these players that'll burn long into the future. That's the kind of impact a coach can have.

Look for all the **little things** in a coach (or as much as you can get), and not just someone looking to win or just have fun.

Then, and only then, will you see a coach with true power and the potential for a **BIG IMPACT.**

SECRET #21

The secret to successful coaching—in sports and in business—lies not in the pursuit of winning alone but in the profound impact a coach has on the players. True success is measured by the coach's commitment to developing minds, instilling values, promoting equal opportunities, and prioritizing the individual and collective growth of every player, creating a lasting impact that extends well beyond the scoreboard.

22

CRUISE CONTROL

Cruise control is dangerous.

In a car. In our work lives. In our relationships. In our physical fitness levels. In our free time. In our political affiliations. In our community involvement.

No joke—it's a killer.

I discovered the link the other day while on a long trip. My right foot was aching and I set the cruise control to give my foot a break.

Fifteen minutes later *a **LOT had changed.***

My mind was less active. My head had settled in to the head rest. My eyes had started getting droopy. I felt my body getting lower into the seat.

I felt like I was falling into a trance—like I was being lulled to sleep.

I recognized how *comfortable* I had gotten so quickly that I shook my head and I immediately sat up. I rolled the windows down to get some fresh air, and I promptly turned the cruise control right back off.

Then, I literally just sat there thinking about how quickly that could have gone bad.

And, then I thought about how we all use **cruise control** when we get tired in our lives. It's necessary at times—but we can't just keep it there, as that's even more dangerous.

Think about it.

If you're on cruise control **at your job—**

> *You're probably getting left behind.*
> *You probably aren't interested in learning new tools or taking on new projects.*
> *You're probably not actively looking for ways to make things better.*
> *You probably don't go out of your way to help those above or below you.*

If you're on cruise control **in your relationships—**

> *Somebody, somewhere is feeling neglected.*
> *Someone is going to feel under appreciated.*
> *Someone's going to feel like someone else has gotten too comfortable.*

It's the same with our **physical fitness**, our **free time**, our **political affiliations**, and our **community involvement.**

If we just put things on cruise control—

> *We pay the price.*
> *We get complacent.*
> *We lose the capacity to influence change.*

We have to be intentional—with our **thoughts**, with our **actions**, with our **minds**, with our **bodies**...with our **conversations.**

Else, we fall into a dangerous trap—

> *A trap that some people never wake from.*
> *A trap that holds you down.*
> *A trap that holds you back.*
> *A trap that can lull you to sleep.*
> *A trap that can ultimately kill whatever ambitions and dreams you had for yourself.*

Be mindful, friends.
Cruise control is dangerous.

SECRET #22

The secret revealed is that relying on cruise control, whether in driving, work, relationships, or various aspects of life, can be dangerously seductive. It lulls us into a state of complacency, stifling growth, ambition, and the capacity to effect positive change. To avoid this trap, one must remain intentional and mindful, actively engaging in thoughts, actions, and relationships to prevent falling into the perilous comfort of cruise control.

23

THE LEADERSHIP TRIFECTA

What is a leader? What is a follower? What about those that are neither or pretend to be one or the other?

But, first, an important one-liner. A one-liner that'll set the tone for what we're about to cover.

Here it is—

A leader cannot lead followers who won't follow.

I want you to think that one through and move forward once you realize how much that statement matters. It matters because leading people who have no interest in following you is a zero-sum game.

In this chapter we'll explore the trifecta of leadership relating to teams (this can be a two-person team, ten-thousand person team or anything in between or larger).

 The trifecta includes **leaders, followers** and —*here's a new term for you*—**disaffiliates.**

A leader is someone who finds a way—

To lead.
To influence.

To shape.
To enable.
To care.

Leadership is a mindset and an active, ongoing role that evolves over time.

It's not a tangible thing.

And, importantly, being a leader has nothing to do with one's position, title, authority, seniority, or pay grade.

A ***follower*** is someone with an active, engaging role that works independently and with intent to help a team and its leader become the best it can be.

Note that both leaders and followers are active roles.

Now, let's look at the third piece—***disaffiliates.***

A disaffiliate looks like a follower, but is much different. This is someone who is a mindless, thoughtless, robot-like zombie that can be programmed or simply obeys everyone and everything they're told. Often times these people say yes, constantly, and tell others they have good ideas regardless of their real thoughts. *Yes men (or women)* of sorts. Disaffiliates are like speed-bumps, hurdles or road blocks in that they slow down both leading and following roles by not joining in and don't add value beyond being told what to do. Or worse, agreeing to make leaders feel better instead of actually helping in any way.

The vast majority of teams can be divided into this trifecta.
Someone who fills the leader role, those that actively look to help their team by following with intent, and those that mindlessly create obstacles that slow progress.

That said, a good leader can only do **so much** without a person, group, or team that's **willing and able** to follow—actively.

More on the *"willing"* part in a moment.

And yes, many so-called leaders prefer to have only disaffiliates as they merely want to boss people around without anyone questioning them. To say things and have everyone say they're a genius.

It's great for ego, but not for progress.

So let me touch on the *"willing"* part to help illustrate this point.

I say, "willing," because following is a choice:

> *Am I on board?*
> *Is the leader someone I can trust?*
> *Am I willing to do what is asked of me without hassle?*
> *Can I do what is asked of me and add value to the leader's request?*
> *Do I require constant supervision to do the job at hand?*
> *Can I be trusted to do the right thing and complete tasks as required?*
> *Do I have the necessary skills or ability to do what is asked of me?*

If the answer to any of these questions is no, the leader cannot lead effectively, or truly bring out the best in others, regardless of their leadership ability.

Conversely, to lead effectively, a leader must meet criteria that's worth following:

> *Am I someone that can be trusted?*
> *Have I earned the trust of my team?*
> *Am I clear about my expectations of the follower(s)?*
> *Am I communicating clearly and concisely?*

Have I equipped my team with proper training, tools, etc?

Can I trust my team do do the right thing without me being involved?

Am I treating my team with respect and giving them opportunities to excel?

Am I watching out for all problem areas (and obstacles) and trying to remove them?

Again, any "NOs" and conflict arises.
NOs push people towards the disaffiliated realm.

When this occurs, the leadership equation breaks down quickly—
And a leader can't lead and a follower can't follow.

A perfect example of this is on a dance floor. A leader's role changes with every follower they dance with. A follower who fully understands the ins and outs of following is either limited by, or unleashed by, the leader's abilities. A skilled follower can make a poor leader look good for a short period, but it wears on them.

A skilled leader on the dance floor can work wonders with a skilled follower—but then be crippled by someone who has no foundation, or worse, someone who wants to do their own thing.

Leading someone—*or a group*—who won't listen, is exhausting.
Leading a team that pretends to listen or just gives you lip-service is equally destructive to a leader's ultimate success.

Sure, it seems to work in the short run—
But it's not sustainable long-term.

Here's the deal:

> *To be a good leader you must also know what being a good follower is.*

To be a good follower you really should understand what a good
leader does, or what they should do.

The more each side knows about the other the easier it is to be a good teammate.

If you're somewhere in between, you're just making things more difficult for those around you.

> **And that's really what leading and following is—it's a team:**
> *In a work environment, on a dance floor, in a school project, at home between a parent and children. In any situation where someone has to take the lead.*

Leadership is about being responsible and accountable.

Following, effectively, is about holding up your end of the bargain— equipping yourself with necessary skills, doing what needs to be done and speaking up when you need help... in any way.

A great leader who gets put on a team that doesn't want to follow is a recipe for disaster. Same with having a team that's hungry for strong leadership and they're given a *"leader"* who doesn't understand their role.

It's easy to be deflated or want to give up in these situations.
We've all been there—

Sometimes, it's at home.
Sometimes, with a teacher.
Sometimes, just working on a project with a friend.

A couple of old quotes come to mind that help reinforce this:

"Two chiefs and no Indians doth not a team make." —and—
"You can lead a horse to water, but you can't make it drink."

Leaders are everywhere.
So are **followers.** So are **disaffiliates.**

The more each of us learn about our roles in all areas of our lives, the easier all our interactions become.

Most people float in and out of these roles regularly.

A leader at work may also report to others where *they're* a follower—

> *Then go home and be the leader to children in need.*
> *Then go to a yoga class or a dance class where they become a follower.*
> *Then work on a project with a spouse where the role changes frequently.*

If there's no real buy-in as to whatever they're doing or whatever they're a part of, they become a disaffiliate.

Children are typically taught to be compliant, but not good followers. This leads more towards disaffiliation.

Compliance says: do as you're told, or else—
Basically consent and/or conform, or else.

A good follower is taught to follow a particular path or direction and can add to it as needed. A follower can think for themselves while working within a framework.

And no, being a follower is not the same as blindly following someone.

This happens when a person follows a narrow set of inputs and follows *just because.* That's also called *"BSing"* or being sheeple or a lemming.

True followers ask questions, understand and enhance the leaders.

Blind followers are merely "yes" people who contribute by doing with their heads and eyes down as they are often **disaffiliated** with either role.

Hence, being **disaffiliates.**

They really don't care about the outcome or progress, in general.

And, to make matters worse, disaffiliates also include the naysayers who proactively stop progress.

> They are part of the team but they're not leading, nor following—
>   they're merely stopping others from doing either one.
> Objection after objection.
> "Why?" after each request.
> Not accepting blame nor responsibility.
> "Not my problem!" kind of people.
> Always asking questions that create doubt and halt momentum.
> Nothing ever makes sense—and they spend more time being angry
>   or dissatisfied with their situation than helping in any way.
> And, they want to tell others how dissatisfied they are with their
>   leaders and the ones who are following them.

Ultimately, both **leadership** and **true followers** are important and interdependent. You can't have one without the other. And, you need disaffiliates to keep everyone in check.

You have to have balance, else power shifts too quickly without a strong foundation.

An imbalance of power rarely is a good thing.

The next time you find yourself in any of the roles—think it through:

Are you doing your part?
Are they doing their part?
Can you both just dance and enjoy the music—
    or is there static that constantly interrupts progress?

And, sure, there are tons of writings on leadership—
And yes, knowing how to be the best leader you can be is important.

But, again...

> *The best leadership without willing and able followers will never accomplish what it could have. Leading disaffiliates is a losing battle as there's never "buy-in"—and burn out is inevitable.*

And, I'll leave you with one last thought that exemplifies the importance of both leadership and following and how disaffiliation fits in. A statement made by many over the years that somehow still rings true:

"Lead, follow or get out of the way!"

Because, really, you have to fit in somewhere. And they're all important.

SECRET #23

The secret revealed is that effective leadership is not just about the leader but also hinges on the willingness and capability of followers. It emphasizes the dynamic interplay between leaders, true followers who actively contribute, and disaffiliates who hinder progress, highlighting the importance of understanding and embracing these roles for successful collaboration and achievement.

24

PLANTING SEEDS

If patience is a virtue, I'd say we're running out of it.

We, as in the world as a whole.

Instant gratification has found its way to the forefront of society, and unfortunately, it's become the norm.

Fast food. Movies on demand. Instant Messaging. Prepackaged foods. Wire transfers. FaceTime. High-speed internet. Tanning beds. Diet pills. Same-day delivery of this, that, and the other.

Everyone seems to want everything, **NOW!**

So, it's no wonder we have leaders out there trying to make everything happen today. They're running at breakneck speeds as though we're in a race to the finish line—and the finish line's right over there, in sight.

Sprints have their time and place.
Every now and then there's a specific reason to join in and run one. But not regularly. Not for a leader *NOR* their team.

If, instead of having full-grown trees delivered today, we plant seeds, we get a completely different result down the road.

You can't shape and mold full-grown trees without seriously damaging them. If you try to get your desired result quickly you'll inevitably end up breaking limbs and shocking them to the core.

Seeds take much longer, but with care, they become something that grows into exactly what you're wanting.

Think about this from a leadership perspective.

If we think of our words or training as a seed and then plant it in those where we want it to grow, then we have to think like gardeners. As we continue to add additional information and supporting materials it's like adding moisture, nutrients and warmth into the soil and germination occurs.

The more we cover regarding the who, what, why, where, when, and how about whatever it is we're wanting them to learn, the greater the foundation of that seed—as in, the roots will spread far and wide.

As roots are forming, connections are being made and growth occurs —hence the stem shooting up through the ground. Questions, in the form of leaves, will pop up and out. Think of these as solar panels that are fed by a leader's answers.

If the leader's answers are clear—
It's like the sun is shining and growth happens fast.

If the leader's answers are unclear—
It's like a cloudy day and growth is somewhat stagnant.

Leaders have to be mindful of the importance of protecting each of those seeds and nurturing them until they're full grown—

Sometimes it's watering them.
Sometimes it's letting them weather their own storm.

Sometimes it's pruning and cutting things back a bit to help foster growth.

Sometimes it's keeping the weeds away so they remain focused.

Planting seeds is a leadership process that's proven to be effective—
And one that goes against the instant gratification model.

Leaders that use this model know better than to expect things to happen overnight. They're okay with progress over time. They know their role in your growth. They're okay with minor setbacks. They're okay with heading towards a finish line that can't be seen.

Expose seeds to the sun too early or for too long, you'll burn them out.
Keep seeds in the dark, they'll never grow.
Give them too much water early on, they'll drown.
Leave them alone for too long, they'll starve.

Plant your seeds, but be patient.
Growth is imminent, and it's gratifying, but it's not instant.

SECRET #24

The secret to effective leadership lies in embracing the art of planting seeds rather than expecting instant results. Leaders should approach their roles like gardeners, carefully planting seeds of knowledge and guidance, understanding that growth requires patience and nurturing. By protecting and providing clear answers, leaders foster a foundation for sustained growth, acknowledging that true leadership is a process that unfolds over time, not an instant sprint to the finish line.

25

GREAT TEACHERS

We hear about great teachers all the time.

We probably have a few teachers in mind that we'd serve up as teacher of the year.

And, everyone seems to *think* they know what being a great teacher means, but they draw blanks when it comes to explaining it.

So, let's explore:
What makes a great teacher?

The question, itself, is interesting as the answer has two completely different directions it can go in.

One is based on the **administrative tasks and doing things by the book,** and the other is based on **impact to the students.**

Let's start out by defining a teacher as someone who teaches others. This could be in a classroom, in a corporate setting, in a karate class, at a church, at home, as a coach, or just about anywhere else *learning* takes place.

The first part of my answer relates to doing all the little things teachers are **expected** to do.

Examples include:

> *Having a full plan of what's to come,*
> *Laying out expectations and the syllabus,*
> *Being clear about how grades work and how things are graded,*
> *Using bulletin boards,*
> *Using white boards,*
> *Having worksheets ready,*
> *Having complete control over your classroom 100% of the time,*
> *Using every second of your time with students to ensure they're learning,*
> *Teaching students to be respectful and compliant,*
> *Always having assignments, quizzes and tests graded immediately,*
> *Having grades posted online the second they're completed,*
> *Ensuring no student is behind in any work at any time,*
> *Updating student progress and having working plans on a weekly basis to address any deficiencies,*
> *Having minimum numbers of passing grades.*

The second part of my answer relates to ***doing whatever it takes to connect with students and make an impact.***

Examples include:

> *Spending time getting to know students,*
> *Inspiring them based on something they know or like and tailoring lessons to them,*
> *Finding ways to incorporate building self-confidence into the curriculum,*
> *Writing notes of encouragement to students who may be struggling,*
> *Writing notes of praise to those you see have done exceptional things,*
> *Calling students out—in a good way—and showcasing them in front of others,*
> *Getting truly excited when someone "gets it" or shows they understand,*

Accepting students for who they are and helping them connect with, and form relationships, with others,
Helping others to see that it's okay to cheer for classmates,
Getting to know both strengths and weaknesses and helping the class to utilize, or overcome them,
Treating students like they matter,
Using real-life examples of how to use what they're learning, and
Helping the class connect material with what they see in the real world.

Both paths make for a ***great teacher,*** but they're different.
Oh. So. Different.

To administrators, if you do everything in the first path, you'd be considered great. On paper, you'd meet the expectations and other teachers might even look to you as an example. You might win some awards to show others it can all be done. Your peers will look to you for help on *"how to do it all."*

And, they're not wrong.
It's just one way to look at it.

In fact, you could do all those things and not actually connect with your students. But, you'd be considered "great" to some.

Now, you could do all those things **AND** do everything in the second path as well. In other words, they're mutually exclusive. You don't need one to do the other.

Both result in being great, but you could do either one and still be *"great"*—it just depends on what matters to you.

If you're a teacher and it matters more to you what your peers and your bosses think, then you'll gravitate towards the first path. It just is.

Again, not right or wrong.

But, if you're more concerned about **making an impact** on someone, then you'll gravitate towards the second path.

Rarely will you find someone that does both with exceptional proficiency, but I'd argue that both could be considered *great* teachers.

Personally, I'm a big fan of the second path—*making an impact.*

I understand the bureaucratic processes but I don't see it as a replacement for what truly matters.

Learning often takes place when someone is interested in something AND they like the person who's teaching.

The teachers I remember are always the ones who made an impact on me in some form or fashion. And, it never had to do with the administrative stuff.

Doesn't matter if it's a 3rd grader, a middle schooler, someone in high school, a grad school student or someone in the workplace—if you start with taking an interest in your students, the potential for making an impact and truly connecting dramatically increases.

But, that might not be what matters to you.

And I won't knock it because, like I said, those that just do the first path are also considered **great teachers.**
It's just a different flavor of great.

Impact matters to me—
And therefore, the second path is, by far, my recommendation.

SECRET #25

The secret revealed is that the essence of a great teacher lies in a dual perspective. One path involves fulfilling administrative duties meticulously, meeting expectations, and being recognized by peers and superiors. The other, more profound path centers on making a lasting impact by connecting with students, understanding their individuality, and fostering an environment that goes beyond bureaucratic processes. Both paths can lead to greatness, but the choice depends on what truly matters to the teacher, whether it's meeting administrative criteria or making a meaningful impact on students' lives.

26

PROFESSIONAL STUPIDITY

There's a large class of people, worldwide, who put extra-ordinary faith and trust into people who boast their *higher education* degrees.

As it relates, I have a series of thoughts and an important question for you:

Is it professional stupidity, willful ignorance, or something else?

A postsecondary degree does not guarantee knowledge, wisdom, credibility, nor anything of the sort. It just means that people expect it.

Conversely, having no degree—*or anything in between*—does not guarantee the *LACK OF* knowledge, wisdom, credibility or anything of the sort.

It just means that people don't expect it.

So what happens when those we expect to have all those things don't actually have it *AND* they're in charge of something?

We get misled. Deceived. Hoodwinked. Misinformed.

It happens all the time, mind you.
*And, it's a reflection of society's **lack of education... about education.***

First, you need to know that learning has nothing to do with a class-room.

Oh, you're told it does, but it really doesn't.

And, you're told that having a degree will make you smarter—but it really doesn't.

If taught correctly, anything, anywhere, can be your classroom.

> *Can you learn in a classroom? Of course.*
> *Can you learn in a bathroom? Of course.*
> *Can you learn on the streets? Of course.*

Once you understand the limitations of what is actually taught in the classrooms—*especially in the cookie-cutter programs that are aimed at maximizing profits and minimizing knowledge*—you'll start to get it.

Let's look at a few examples.

You'd think medical doctors have extensive training in the nutritional benefits of food, right? Turns out, that's far from the truth. Most medical programs offer less than twenty contact hours of training—yep, that's right, less than half of a week.

You'd think veterinarians have extensive training in pet nutrition, right? Turns out, that's also far from the truth. Most vet programs have little to *NO* training on nutrition whatsoever. Interestingly, though, there's a program to become a veterinary nutritionist—
and it's three years of specific training.

Now, what about scientists?

I mean, really, if we should trust the outcomes, we should expect:

Major regulations on the integrity of findings,
Full disclosure of all facets of experiments including ingredients,
Traceability into all funding sources, and
Multiple peer-reviewed sign-offs from non-stakeholder entities.

But, of course, that's not the case either—*as that just doesn't seem to exist anymore.*

Oh, and don't get me wrong—
I'm not saying a doctor, veterinarian, scientist, or any other professional that falls into this category can't have the knowledge, wisdom, or credibility as they absolutely can—I'm just saying it's not the norm as it's not part of the *education* process that's been set up.

Each one of them would have to go out of their way and obtain the knowledge a different route. And, many of them do—not the majority though.

Here's what this means.

At no point should we trust anyone **just because** they have a degree or a title or some type of official credentials.

Trust is earned.

Trust is open and honest and based in character.

Our world would be infinitely easier to navigate if all those that are leading others actually cared enough to be up front and honest about their own limitations and knowledge base.

The number of people that make decisions based on someone's "credentials" is absolutely astounding—in as much as those who are not credentialed—who **have** the knowledge, wisdom, and credibility often get ridiculed and brushed out of the way by society, as a whole.

"Professional stupidity," as I wrote it, is really what happens when a professional stops "learning" and refuses to continue their education or stay up on current topics once they become a professional.

*This happens in every industry—**but it's not everyone**.*

"Willful ignorance," as I wrote it, is when people have been presented all the information they need to be truly *"educated"* on a topic—**and they ignore it.** *This happens often with politicians.*

So what do we do?

Stop assuming anyone called a doctor knows everything. *Just stop.*

Stop assuming anyone called a vet knows everything about animals. *Just stop.*

Stop assuming science-based findings that flash on your TV or computer are what they say they are—and were properly done in the context of true science. *Just stop.*

> *Educate yourself on the issues.*
> *Educate yourself on what it is you're talking to "professionals" about.*
> *Educate yourself prior to making decisions, and, if you feel the lack of knowledge crushing—don't stop and simply hand over your powers to those with **higher education.***

By the way, the term 'higher education' is such a farce *as it positions that form of education above everything else and that's simply not the case.*

I respect the discipline it takes to go through those programs—but I don't blindly give credit where it's not earned.

Last, this really goes for any titled **professional—**
Not just those who have letters after their names.

I'm talking managers, supervisors, executives, agents, mayors, governors, principals, professors, and judges. Oh, and there's lawyers, nurses, pastors, teachers, police officers, coaches, superintendents, journalists, athletic directors, etc.

Just because someone's in a titled position doesn't make them the authority, it just simply states they have assumed or inferred power over something.

Make people earn your respect by delivering information and services that are truly helpful to you, not just the *"way it's always been"* or the current *"protocol"* or some other cockamamie answer that patronizes you.

No ones expects any professional to **know it all—**
But they dang sure expect them to be resourceful and honest about their knowledge, wisdom, character and credibility.

When you don't know, you don't know—
Be humble enough to say you'll look into it and provide your best recommendation at some predetermined time.

And, be open to the fact that what you learned in school **might not** be what the answer is today—**and be willing to change.**
I mean, really, that's the kind of leadership we all need.

That's the kind of leader we should be.

Hold people accountable.
Hold yourself accountable.

Be wise enough to question all things going on around you—
And then sort out your answers.

You have to answer for you and your team.
Don't just go with the first thing that makes you *feel* good.

Rarely is life that simple.

Here's the bottom line for leaders...

When we all have to depend on each other—
It's nice to know we have people we can depend on.

And, it's nice to know that we can be one of those people too.

SECRET #26

The secret revealed is that professional credentials, titles, and degrees don't automatically guarantee knowledge, wisdom, or credibility. Blindly trusting professionals based on their formal education can lead to deception and misinformation, emphasizing the importance of individuals educating themselves on issues and questioning authority figures. The key is not to assume that someone in a professional role knows everything but to evaluate their knowledge, character, and credibility through earned respect and accountability.

27

LET PEOPLE BE HEARD

There was a time when I had to make and set agendas. Every topic had a time limit, or—*if it was people*—each person had a time limit.

It was like this in college. It was like this when I worked with missile systems for the Govt. It was like this as a consultant for the V.A. It was like this in Congressional briefings. It was like this in my MBA program. And, it was like this in my own company.

Everyone's voice mattered—but so did the clock.

Often, a timekeeper would be assigned to keep everyone on or ahead of schedule—

I've been the timekeeper.
I've had to assign the timekeeper.
And I've been held to times by the timekeeper.

I get it.

People had to prepare for their *limited time* and, hopefully, the constraint allowed enough time for what needed to be covered.

This works well—until it doesn't.
I mean, look, sometimes the time allotted doesn't matter.

The issue or topic is pretty black and white and it is what it is.
For those, oftentimes, time limits wouldn't be reached and either everyone goes home early or someone else is allotted more time *(not very often—on that part).*

But, when the topic **MATTERS,** it's absolutely appalling when someone says any of the following:

> *"Sorry, your time has expired."*
> *"We're going to have to move on to the next item."*
> *"We'll have to follow up on this topic at our next meeting when we have more time."* ... or ...
> *"I'm gonna have to cut you off right there as we have to go to a commercial."*

How about ANY of these, instead:

> *"Right here. Right now. Let's make it happen."*
> *"Let's settle this before the end of the meeting."*
> *"Let's talk it out while we're still on the topic."*
> *"What else should we know?"*
> *"What have we missed?"*
> *"Let's keep this going."*
> *"Why can't we make a decision now?"*
> *"Who else needs to be involved?"*
> *"Keep going, this is important."*
> *"Let's get to the bottom of it once and for all."*
> *"Let's just remove all other topics and focus in on this and only this."*

You know, things like that.

*It takes **guts** to rock the boat.*
*It takes **courage** to stand up when everyone else is sitting.*
*It takes a **true leader** to recognize when exceptions need to be made—and to make them happen for the greater good.*

Cutting people off when they're passionate about something rarely works out in the end. The *moment* is lost and will most likely never surface again.

Stopping progress for the sake of an agenda or a schedule is an awful way to conduct any business that *needs* to be done.

Claiming someone's time is up just to appease everyone else has short-term gains—that degrade the overall environment long-term.

Truth is, sometimes when the time is up, it takes a **special kind of leader** to recognize the importance and give respect where respect is due.

This is where leaders have the opportunity to **extend times** and let people go on and on—**IF** their message is worthwhile and relevant OR the topic is timely and warrants further discussion immediately.

Now, more than ever, when the right message needs to be shared, we all need to put our agendas away and simply...

Let people be heard.

SECRET #27

The secret revealed is that while time limits and agendas are necessary in various professional settings, true leadership recognizes when exceptions need to be made for the greater good. Cutting people off when they're passionate about important topics can hinder progress, and allowing worthwhile discussions to continue beyond allotted time fosters a more respectful and productive environment.

28

BUS DRIVERS

L eaders that ride the struggle-bus are more common than you think—especially when it comes to numbers.

Not knowing how to use them.
Not understanding their importance.
Not knowing how to separate things out.
Heck, not knowing how or when to collect them.

Instead of just being a passenger, let's re-imagine our role.
Let's change the name from the struggle-bus to the number-bus and, since we can, let's promote ourselves to become the **bus driver.**

First thing we'll do is paint five big letters on the side of it that read:

WGMGI

Most people won't understand it, but we will.
Those five letters stand for five critical words:

 **What Gets Measured Gets Improved**

Those five words encapsulate the branding we want our number-bus to communicate.

Second, we embrace the notion that numbers are everywhere.

How many times this.
How many times that.

Once you start seeing things in numbers, you notice that they're everywhere. As such, here are some typical examples of how numbers are used to measure things.

How many seconds.
How many responses.
How many opens.
How many strikes.
How many touchdown passes.
How many wins, losses, tackles, missed field goals, greens in
*   regulation, putts, hits, kills, and, of course, how many likes.*

There's more:

How many comments, deletions, emails, customers, interactions,
*   deaths, inquiries, items scanned per minute, times you're late,*
*   clicks per day, reps you perform, ads per day, and what's your*
*   cost per conversion...*

The list goes on and on.

And, for things that can't easily be counted: **no problem—**
Find similarities or groupings of some type and assign it a number, then
count.

Once you have a count, you can **measure.**
When you measure, you **focus your attention.**
Where you focus your attention, **improvements are almost certain** to
happen.

Now, although critical for anyone in management—this thought process is a must for coaches, teachers, parents and those of us interested in self-improvement.

In other words, if you want to make a single thing better, *measure it—* and watch it improve. *It's an easy strategy.*

Know this, though:

> *Once you shift your focus to some new area, something else usually changes.*

Think of it as a new bus route.

Oftentimes, it's a trade off.

You choose to spend two hours a day writing, but to do so you have to forego your gym time. Or, you stop eating out so much, but to eat at home you must now shop more, spend more time preparing food, cooking and cleaning up.

It just is.

This is why change is hard—but it's also why it works.

When you measure things, you get a whole new outlook on what's possible with effort.

You see, our **society loves to measure things** and show statistics. PowerPoint and Excel made graphs fun and easy years ago and, ever since, people have been plugging in data that makes for a more appealing story.

Nowadays, you can't visit a website without seeing some type of chart or graph that helps someone's narrative.

It's said that **87% of all statistics are made up** *(just like that one)* and I believe it.

And, because of that, marketers, worldwide, use numbers to convince us:

> *That "everyone's doing it," or*
> *That "65% of Americans agree," or*
> *"4 out of 5 dentists" (that we paid) recommend this product.*

If it's something you want to measure and improve, do so and watch how quickly you get wherever you want to go.

 Your numbers. You benefit.

If it's someone else's numbers and you're being told or sold something, *know how easy it is to manipulate data* and use it in a way that appeals to your emotional and rational brain at the same time.

 Their numbers. They benefit.

Ultimately it's this:

> *Most people want to do what others are doing and merely follow*
> *along. It doesn't make it right or wrong, but it really does set*
> *people up to be controlled by **what they're told** the masses are*
> *doing.*

Many people look to the TV or internet to see what people are doing—and they start doing that thing just because they think others must know what they're doing.

Turns out, that's not the case at all.

Most people are just lazy and do whatever's easy and whatever the *norm* is. That's why marketing and the use—*or misuse*—of numbers is so powerful.

In the long run, if you're not aware of how numbers can be used both for your benefit—*and then against society in whole*—you'll lose.

To summarize:

As the *WGMGI bus driver,* you get to map out your destination—

> *You get to choose your routes and pick up whatever numbers you want.*
> *Go too fast and you'll miss things.*
> *Go too slow, and you'll fall behind.*

Figure out how to measure whatever it is you want to measure—
And you'll improve whatever it is you want to improve.

SECRET #28

The secret revealed is that measuring and focusing on numbers leads to improvement, and this principle is crucial not only for management but for coaches, teachers, parents, and those interested in self-improvement. However, this chapter also highlights the caution to be aware of how numbers can be manipulated, emphasizing the importance of digging deep to find true numbers for informed decision-making.

29

STRATEGIC ALLIANCES

One of the most important concepts one could learn in business school relates to collaboration— *With other businesses.*

If you position your company right, set your company up in the best possible way, do your research, and find other businesses that complement yours, you have the makings for a powerful *strategic alliance.*

Right?

You can share risks and costs, leverage strengths and minimize weaknesses, and you could alter the perceived capabilities of your company in the eyes of the customer.

With strategic alliances, you give your company a competitive advantage in the marketplace—and the synergies that can come of it are often immeasurable.

That's the kind of stuff you learn in school.

Here's what you won't learn.

The people we meet, work with, seek out, and share time with all have value.

To simplify, we'll call these people our **connections.**

Each of our connections has the potential to connect us with their **knowledge, resources, strengths, tips,** *and* **wisdom.**

We have the potential to do the same.

If we look at each of our connections as a potential **STRATEGIC ALLIANCE,** our worlds expand exponentially.

Here's some context, a framework, and some thoughts to consider as you go.

I have a background that's filled with diverse experiences, jobs, and education. Everything I've done, learned, been a part of, seen, felt, worked through, and lived becomes what I bring to the table.

It's all inside of me. It's in my head and in the very fabric of the breaths I breathe.

The manager I just met at the hotel—guess what? He has a background filled with diverse experiences, jobs, and education.

Everything he's done, learned, been a part of, seen, felt, worked through, and lived is what he brings to the table.

A video camera there in the lobby would capture two guys, empty-handed, standing, and talking—separated by a seemingly empty table.

The camera, itself, won't see all of what's **inside.**
What we *"brought to the table."*

That part is for us to discover—*if we so choose.*

You see, each of us has an opportunity to intentionally do something ***extraordinary.***

Ordinary would simply be to handle whatever business needs to be handled and walk away from the table.

Being extra says we want more. Something ***extra,*** if you will. To discover something interesting about the other person.

Being intentional says we make it a point to genuinely connect using small talk.

Small talk allows for context:

> *Perhaps the reason why you're at the hotel.*
> *Perhaps something interesting you've seen or experienced since being at the hotel.*
> *Perhaps something about your family and how many of you there are staying.*

Every bit of information either one of you shares at this point has the potential to unlock something else.

If we're actively listening, we're ***keying*** in on words and asking thoughtful questions.

We're getting someone to peel a layer or two off their proverbial onion.

It's how we learn about what someone else has ***in their head—***

> *Their story.*
> *The history of* ***them.***

Or, again, to see what they ***bring to the table.***

If they're a good conversationalist **AND** they're interested in you and your story, they'll ask questions.

But, be patient. They may still just be excited that someone cared enough to ask them.

Or, if you see the potential alliance right away, you can speak up for yourself to help the questioning process *move along.*

An example might be that the hotel manager reveals that he has a major staffing problem right now. You may know someone who has a staffing company or you may have some talented friends looking to change careers and you offer up some information.

 The "key" here is to have meaningful conversations with people—and actually get to know them and their story.

And when you discover the differences—you know, the things they know that you don't, or the experiences they've had that you haven't, or whatever—you celebrate those things.

> *You talk to them and ask questions.*
> *You nod along and smile.*
> *You take an interest in whatever that thing is they're talking about and you learn about it for their sake.*

Each time you do this, you align with someone new.
Strategically, you gain an asset.

For some small subset of something in the world, you gain a new mentor. Someone who knows more than you about something.

A "business partner" of sorts, without having to do business with them. Someone who can provide you fresh insight.

AND, you learn something new.

Over the years I've created hundreds of **Strategic Alliances** with people I value, trust, and look up to.

Connections, if you will, that have shared their knowledge, time, and resources with me to improve and enhance my life—just as I've done for them and theirs.

For this to work, you can't ***use*** people.
You have to genuinely put the time in—

> *To care. To show up. To invite them into your world.*
> *To take an interest in whatever it is that interests them.*
> *To talk to them away from the table where you did your first*
>   ***business,*** *whatever that business was.*

And to create value, long-term, for THEM in whatever way only YOU can.

Strategic alliances between people are powerful—
They take time, but they matter.

We all need different perspectives.

We all have something someone else needs—
And we all need something someone else has.

We all need to be seen, heard, and connected with.
We all need someone else to align with to help us along in life.

That's what strategic alliances do.

Be intentional.
Align with people you like *AND* that are different than you.
Bring value to the table.
Share and share alike.

Team with others.
Ask questions and talk openly.
Get excited about someone else's experiences and help *THEM* grow.

 You may not need these people today, but you just might tomorrow. *And, believe me, you don't want to go digging your well the day you're thirsty.*

I mean, really, here's the deal:

> *If you want to be a leader that continuously pools resources, gains knowledge, accesses new technologies, and listens to wisdom of those who've been there and done that—create strategic alliances.*

If you just want to **Network,** then collect names, business cards, and shake hands with people—the world is filled with people like that who want to make it look like they care, but don't.

> **Don't just look to "do business" with people—connect with them. On a level that means something.**

Do this and you'll start to look at people in a whole new way—
And you'll probably end up treating them better as well.

That's a side effect of thinking someone's *valuable*—
And, remember, everyone is.

And, start today, not tomorrow.
Really.

There are tons of people out there who can make your world infinitely better *(and certainly more interesting)*.

They come in all shapes, sizes, colors, races—
And with varying education levels.
And they need *someone like you* to do the same for theirs.

Strategic alliances—
Because we're all better, together.

SECRET #29

Leadership is about creating strategic alliances with people, not just businesses. By intentionally connecting with others and genuinely getting to know their stories, experiences, and perspectives, leaders can unlock valuable assets and resources. These alliances are built on mutual respect, trust, and the exchange of knowledge and support, ultimately leading to personal and professional growth for all involved. The key is to be genuine, patient, and open-minded, and to recognize the inherent value in EVERY individual connection.

30

ROOT CAUSES

I f every problem was exactly as it appeared, our world would be boring.

We'd see a problem, fix it, and move on.

No further thought.
No expert opinions.
No additional analysis.
No thinking our way through the system.

Wham-bam-thank-you-ma'am... we'd be in and out of broken things and back to work.

But, things aren't always what they seem.

I mean, sure, if we're lucky, that thing that's broken is all that needs fixing.

But, if we're not, the brokenness kicks off a sleuth-like series of discoveries where we continuously make connections with bewilderment.

"Well, no wonder..." is a common phrase starter at this point.
"A-ha" moments are frequent and welcomed.

 **This all happens once we discover that the broken piece is part of a larger system.**

Point in case, our fan pulley recently broke on our zero-turn mower and we found the pieces in our yard, behind us.

We thought we knew what had happened, but we were wrong.
Upon further review, the broken fan pulley was just the tip of the iceberg.

Turns out, the fan pulley is part of a full system that broke down.

The *"system"* included a broken motor mount bolt.
Finding that bolt led us to a broken frame mount that knocked off the foot pedal to lift the deck.

At this point, we noticed a lug nut had sheared off causing a wobble in the wheel that then turned in. The wheel being turned in put extra pressure on the pulley fans that ended up snapping on both sides. The pulley fans snapping caused the drive belt to slip, rip and tear into pieces—all in a matter of about three seconds.

So, here's why this matters.

If we look to merely fix the *thing* that's visibly broken, we often miss the opportunity to deepen our understanding of things and/or relationships.

Root cause is important.
Whether things or people—we have to answer the question, "why?"

Why things break has to do with—

> *What it is,*
> *What it's made out of,*
> *What it's being used for,*
> *What it's connected to,*
> *What the expected or maximum load is, and*
> *If it's maintained properly.*

Oftentimes, we don't know all the answers nor think about the *why* before the break.

Relationships break for many of the same reasons—

>*What type of relationship,*
>*What it's made out of (or based on),*
>*What it's being used for,*
>*What it's connected to,*
>*What the expected or maximum load is, and*
>*If it's maintained properly.*

It's far better to understand, build connections and ask questions during the *maintenance phase* to prevent breakdowns that affect everything in the system.

And, if we're being honest, many of the systems out there are built *without* the right pieces.

That applies to both *products and people—*
As well as a ton of other current **hot topics.**

Some might even be designed to *maximize breakage.*

Best to check it, before you wreck it.

SECRET #30

The secret revealed is that fixing a visible problem is often just addressing the tip of the iceberg, and true understanding and prevention come from investigating the deeper roots within a larger system. Whether dealing with machinery or relationships, a focus on root causes, understanding components, connections, and regular maintenance is crucial for long-term success and stability.

31

WHAT IF I'M WRONG?

D o you ever ask yourself, *"What if I'm wrong?"*

If so: great.
If not: you should.

Being wrong about something is human. We're all wrong, frequently, about everything from our thoughts, our beliefs, our assumptions, our perspectives, our judgments, our actions, our reactions and the way we speak or act towards someone.

Ugh!

A lot of the time this is based on either a lack of information or what I call *"passed-down information"* from generation to generation and it just is.

> *Sometimes it's cultural,*
> *Sometimes an old wives-tale,*
> *Sometimes it's just an unquestioned legend,*
> *Sometimes it's from an old book,*
> *Sometimes it's from a teacher or a pastor or an authority figure, and*
> *Sometimes, it's a friend.*

It could be how that information was presented to us, what information was added or left out, and/or how we feel about the person delivering it—in other words, are they a so-called *trusted* source?

As a whole, we're wrong probably a lot more than we know about.

And, here's the beauty—most people don't want to know the real *truths* for fear that it might reveal they're wrong. Often, we'll merely seek out others or other information that confirms what we were hoping to see *(aka confirmation bias)*.

Sound familiar?

I've done this and so have you. We all have—*but that's not the true issue at play.*

Here's a few examples of what people are regularly wrong about: *diets, exercise, medicine, air quality, food, politics, global agendas, electricity, how our bodies work, cell-phone radiation, chemicals, space, credit, nutrition, geoengineering, recycling, the banking industry, history, ingredients, climate change, drugs, and, of course, religion.*

Where being wrong becomes interesting is with **awareness.**

It's the moment of realization that we're wrong, or that we might be, and how we **react** from there.

 **Keyword: react.**

In other words, it's when we analyze the situation for what it is.

Being wrong about something is uncomfortable. Admitting to yourself you were wrong is hard, but it's important. And, sometimes we don't know we're wrong so we have to really dig deep. We have to think about our assumptions or beliefs and then create a list of other possibilities.

What do we do from there?

When stuck in the **unknown** realm, it's best to test alternative beliefs to see if they **might** be true. Treat them like they're an experiment. Until you're willing to see if these alternatives play out, you don't know if you were right or wrong all along.

But you have to be **willing** to consider the possibilities.

When you determine you were wrong, accepting responsibility for the wrong doing is the critical next step—and it's often a sign of maturity *(regardless of age)*.

*And, yes, accepting that you're wrong takes **courage.***

In other words, the *wrong* has to be **clear to YOU** before you can make it clear to others. Separate your action (whatever it was you did wrong or your belief about something) from who you are (your character) and try to figure out *why* it was a mistake in the first place.

To say it differently, you have to **own up** to whatever it was.

What can you or did you learn?

Making a mistake doesn't mean you're weak or stupid—it simply means you're human.

Now, clearly, there are varying levels of wrongs or mistakes that I'm talking here. I'm not talking about wrongs that are illegal, as those are their own debate in and of themselves.

I'm talking about everyday mistakes or wrongdoings or beliefs about the world or narratives around us.

Okay, now, back to it...

When you discover you're wrong and you want to make things right, there's *five steps* you can take.

1.   **Self admission** *(taking responsibility for your actions, thoughts, assumptions, etc.).*

2.   **Admission to those affected** *(don't make excuses or use words like, "but").*

3.   **Apologize,** *sincerely (if warranted), for the action and any problems or hurt feelings it may have caused.*

4.   **Validate** *feelings of those affected (including your own).*

5.   **Move forward with understanding.**

We're all wrong, regularly, but we need to be able to analyze or question our own beliefs and actions in a way that gives us feedback. Without feedback, it's really hard to *discover* anything.

The more we *discover,* the more we realize we may be making **invalid** or **incomplete assumptions** about things that shape our days—or what we tell others.

These are big moments in our lives. Moments where we have to step back, take a deep breath and think. Again, it's not fun for anyone to realize they've made mistakes, but it's part of life and something we have to deal with.

Our coping (the dealing with it part) needs to have an exit plan at the end of the day.

And, here's a big one:

Our views today may not be what they are tomorrow, nor the next day—and that's okay.

We may learn things today that reveal that we were wrong about something and it's up to us to analyze our decisions and acknowledge that *thing* as part of those five steps I just mentioned. Some things we're wrong about—*like food or medicine or what we consume online*—may only affect us, so the process goes faster. But it still needs to be addressed.

> ***Being wrong doesn't mean you're weak—***
> *It means you made a decision that you can now learn from.*

Did you catch that?

Making the same wrong decision over and over is a different story and may require ***intervention*** of some type.

You can't beat yourself up over being wrong. When you admit and apologize for your mistakes, you show you're **human** and you **care** about others. You make others feel better about their mistakes. You become more **trusted.** You become **real.** You earn **respect.** You show **humility.**

Don't try to be perfect—perfect doesn't exist.

*Be the best version of you that **learns, tries, makes mistakes, admits mistakes, learns again and moves forward.***

People that hide mistakes, refuse to take responsibility, or worse—*blame others,* make situations very difficult to navigate and leave everyone puzzled. Not only does it become uncomfortable, working with people you don't trust makes life miserable.

Working with people who regularly blame others and refuse to take responsibility for anything *degrades any environment* they're in.

Oh, and one last thing.

Everything in this chapter is **action-oriented**—meaning, it was being wrong after *doing or learning something.*

Doing **nothing** is a much bigger problem. Inaction based on indecision often leaves everyone out to dry.

No lessons can be learned from doing the right thing *nor* from doing the wrong thing—*when NOTHING is done.*

Do something... right or wrong. Just do something.

And, when you come to the moments when you recognize that you were wrong, or that you might be—*relax. This is where growth happens, your understanding of the world expands, and you start to see the world with a different lens.*

SECRET #31

The secret revealed is that being wrong is a human experience, but the true measure of growth lies in how leaders react to and learn from their mistakes. Embracing self-awareness, admitting errors, apologizing sincerely, and taking action to understand and correct one's wrongs not only fosters personal growth but also builds trust, respect, and authenticity in relationships.

32

RELAY RACES

Picture being in a relay race.
The baton is in your hand and you're rounding the last corner.

You've got to pass it off to your teammate and you can see them getting ready. You know what's about to happen as you've done it a hundred times.

By the time you get there they'll be **up to speed** and ready to take over while in **full stride.** You'll do an underhand handoff, they'll reach back with their palm down, and there'll be a smooth transition. Right?

You know the process. I know the process.

When we're physically on the track, it just makes sense. These are the things we work on and practice. We prepare for this very moment. I mean, really—**the way you hand things off matters.**

But, you know what we don't do?

We don't spend enough time on the process of handing things off in the workplace. As such, let's take a moment to think this through from a leadership perspective.

What kinds of batons get passed?

Let's just start with the biggest one—**knowledge transfer.**

This one alone directly affects all types of leaders including small business owners, front-line managers, and teachers.

It's when we pass information, expertise and skills on to others. It's the actual process of getting it from one person to the other, successfully.

Other typical ones include **decision-making authority** and **responsibilities**—*when we empower others to make decisions or take on new tasks, projects, or roles.*

> **It's a hand-off from someone who has the authority or the responsibility—and they're giving it to someone else.**

Before I go much farther—*because there's definitely more examples*—let's talk about why this matters.

 First—how we transfer anything matters.

We don't just **throw the baton** and hope for the best.
We show up, expectedly, with the baton and they anticipate what comes next.

As the receiver, they need to be actively engaged and ramping up in some form or fashion **PRIOR** to the handoff.

Then, we run with our partner until such time as they're *"up to speed."* Then, we place it in their hands and we let them take over.

Second—as leaders, we watch.

We don't just hand things off and dip out of the race.
We let that person *"run with it"* and do their thing—but the baton matters until it reaches the finish line, or until it gets passed to the next person.

If the baton gets dropped, we need to make sure the person carrying it is okay—

> Do they need help?
> Do they need to exit the race?
> Does someone else need to take over from there?
> And, of course, the question that'll linger for leaders, why'd they
>   drop it?

And last—we need to be aware of who's next in line—

> Are they prepared for what's coming?
> Do they understand their role?
> Do they understand what happens when they get the baton?
> Do they know who's depending on them?

So, what other examples are there for when we "hand things off" as leaders?

> How about when we share tools and resources,
> When we introduce team members to key stakeholders,
> When we bring in new hires,
> When we transition from one employee to another due to
>   promotions, retirement, or any upcoming event where change
>   is imminent,
> When there's growth and we need people to take over on new
>   areas,
> When we introduce new material for a test or new requirements
>   for a build.

In all of these examples—*it matters how we pass the baton.*

Ask these questions the next time you want to transfer something to someone else:

> *Does that person know we're on the same team and that we're running the same race?*
> *Do I understand the best way to pass the baton?*
> *At what point do I pass the baton?*
> *How can I prepare the next person to best "receive" the baton?*
> *Where is the baton going from here?*
> *Who is responsible if the baton doesn't make it all the way around?*

If we're all on the same team, it matters.
We all have a vested interest in the baton.
We all have to do our part to make sure it keeps moving forward—regardless of what *"it"* is.

We all have to understand our own roles and help those around us so that we can win as a team.

And we all lose if the baton gets dropped, lost, or broken.

Run your race, but know this—you can't run forever.

As a part of a team, *YOU have to do YOUR part and do it well.*

Your team is watching and they're depending on you.
And, as a leader, you need to make sure others are ready for the next hand-off as well.

All that said, let's take a breather and do a quick recap before the next lap.

Here goes...

Prepare your team—

> To look out for one another,
> To work as a team,
> To ramp up their skills,
> To not slow each other down,
> And to take things in stride to keep your baton moving forward.

Do these things well and your team will be *one for the record books.*

Oh, and your next race... is about to begin.
On your mark, get set...

SECRET #32

The secret to effective leadership lies in mastering the art of handing things off smoothly, just like passing a baton in a relay race. Whether it's knowledge, responsibilities, or decision-making authority, the process matters. Leaders must ensure that their team members are actively engaged, prepared for their roles, and supported throughout the handoff process, fostering a culture of teamwork and continuous progress. By understanding the importance of seamless transitions and preparing the next generation of leaders, teams can work together to achieve success in the race towards their goals.

33

INFRINGEMENTS

See if you can make sense of this?

Infringement happens any time we use our *senses* in a way that crosses over to another person.

The way I see it, we have countless choices throughout our day and each decision results in one of three possible outcomes as it relates to the impact on others:

One, it **connects us.**
Two, it **does nothing at all.**
Or, three, it **disconnects us.**

Yep. Just those three outcomes.

I describe this talk as **"Infringement 101"**—and it's about things within your control, not variables you can't control: your skin color, height, age, sex... and yes, I'm aware arguments exist where each of those can be debated, but I digress.

So, I'll say this.

Infringement, as I'm defining it here is all one-sided—*you know, where each of us infringe on others throughout our days*—and does not account for the other side, which is all based on reactions. As leaders, it's important we understand how infringements work both for ourselves **AND** our people, as this topic touches everyone.

Think of infringement as the moment someone else notices you exist and are part of their world.

It's basically an activation of someone else's senses.
It's an encroachment of sorts where you cross paths with another human and they react, respond or judge based on what you present.

Cool! Well, wait. **Which senses?**

The five main ones. **Sight. Smell. Taste. Touch. Hearing.**
—*in no particular order.*

Some would argue *(validly)* there are more senses, but for my take on how they impact each of us I'll stick with the main ones.

Here's my explanation.

If I wear a shirt that has a particular saying on it, and others can see or read it, those three possible outcomes include the following: someone could compliment me *(connect us),* ignore me *(does nothing at all),* or get offended or take it the wrong way *(disconnect us).* By putting that shirt in front of them, I've infringed on their sense of **Sight** and they get to choose their reaction.

I can—*and should*—do what makes me happy (within reason), but I have to be aware of others' beliefs, biases and prejudices and deal with whatever happens by making the choices I do. We all do.

Okay, back to my point.

Other *sight infringements* could include your haircut, makeup, tattoos, pants, shoes, jewelry, piercings, purse, facial hair, phone, glasses, your nails, socks, hats, color choices, etc. And, of course, this also includes things that are extensions of us—a meme you share or some written words in a post or a comment, or your place of residence, your neighborhood, your penmanship, a clean room, a type of car, logos you wear, brands you support, etc.

Each choice has the potential to **connect, be neutral, or disconnect** *us.*

Heck, **affinity marketing** is based on the *"connectedness"* and sense of belonging that people crave and it's extremely powerful as a way of bringing people together.

Oh, and there's a few other **BIG ones** as it relates to **body language** and what people see:

> *A smile,*
> *Folded arms,*
> *Rolling of the eyes,*
> *Eye contact,*
> *Tapping of the toes,*
> *A perplexed look.*

If you want to go *unnoticed, or be neutral,* you'd look at each of those factors and you'd make choices that are **safe**.

If you want to *connect with others*, you'd wear a vintage Buccaneers shirt (any team, really) and a hat to a sports bar in your hometown.

By connecting with some, you'll automatically disconnect with others —perhaps Chiefs fans that are at the next table over?

Now, before I go much further, let me be clear:

I'm not saying **NOT** to infringe—I'm saying with each choice we make, we end up with a ripple effect.

For those that choose **sex appeal**, the connections and disconnections are polarizing. *You'll find the extremes both directions.*

These infringements are what makes life interesting—
Without them, we merely exist.

But you have to choose.

And, I'll say this:

> **Connections are a type of attractant.**
> **Disconnects are a type of turn-off.**

Sometimes a single variable can draw you into someone *(perhaps a smell?)*—or be the exact reason you don't want to be around them *(perhaps a smell?).*

Now, let's move on to another.
The sense of **Smell**—how'd you guess?

Most people have the ability to smell. Some people have **extraordinary** abilities to smell and differentiate all types and sources of smell. Some people are naturally attracted to smells and others are turned off simply by the first *wiff* of something.

Let's explore.

The following is **top of mind smells** we all have choices about that will **infringe on others** we're close to. Type of deodorant, no deodorant at all, hand lotion, body lotion, soaps, perfume, cologne, hair products, our breath, laundry detergent, dryer sheets, recent foods we've eaten, lingering smoke smells, animal smells, and, some things that are extensions of us—the smell in our dwelling (dusty, musty or moldy smells), gases, our garbage, candles, scents, etc.

Now, before you go and say I'm thinking way too much about this, and that it's not that important—focus on **any one** of the variables I just covered within the **smell or sight** realm and test the limits.

Go to an extreme and see if it garners a **connection** or **disconnection**, quickly.

Will it be everyone? No.
But it'll be a lot more than what you might expect.

Some people keep to themselves and don't want to interact at all—no matter how extreme something is. They just let others go by and keep their *"offendedness"* to themselves.

A few more to explore, but I think you get the point.

Taste is a funny one. The foods we eat, the drinks we drink, the substances we consume. The restaurants we choose. The brands we select. The type of cookware we use. What our bowls, cups and plates are made of. Seasonings. Spices. Sweets. Fats.

Over time, our *tastes* change and our taste buds can get damaged in ways that alter our likes and dislikes. Infections, medical conditions, nutrient deficiencies, smoking, medications, radiation exposure, and nerve damage can all affect our taste buds.

So can burning your tongue.

Our tastes influence our decisions on where and what we eat.
Those choices connect us to others who do what we do, make no difference, or disconnect us from others.

"I can't believe you eat at that restaurant—their food is awful!" or

"Ew. He loves mushrooms? I could never be with someone who eats mushrooms!" or

"You drink almond milk too? I love almond milk," or

"I love eating at her house—she's the best cook I've ever met!" or, contrary,

"I hate eating at their house, it's too healthy for me!"

Moving on.

Touch. Oh boy. This one will give you the *"feels."* Texture of clothing, the smooth or rough skin on your hands, how you like your mattress, what type of sheets you like versus the ones you can't sleep on, the softness or firmness of your pillow. How your shoes feel. How firm your skin is. How smooth your skin is to the touch.

The choices you make about materials, lotions, clothing, and anything that others might *touch* can greatly affect the **connect** vs **disconnect** portions of infringement.

When you cross over and **touch others directly**, *this is amplified even more.* Hugs, holding hands with a sibling, a gentle touch on the shoulder, a rough hand, a handshake, a high five, an elbow bump, a chest bump, a warm embrace, a massage, etc. The list could go on and on.

The **moment of impact**—connection, disconnection, or neutral—happens immediately.

A weak handshake turns many people off immediately, and distrust is associated; whereas to others, they think nothing of it.

A friendly hug can get *creepy* just by the amount of pressure or how long it's held.

A well-placed hand on another's in a time of need can have far-reaching effects *(pun intended)*.

Touching a stranger in any way when arguing just might set off a series of terrible events.

And, last, but not least, we have Hearing.

 ***Hearing or Sound,*** can and does infringe on others very quickly. Nearly as quickly as sight, but scientifically proven to be slower.

What we say matters in a number of ways:

The words we use,
The tone we use,
The volume we use,
The speed we use,
The language we use.

The sounds we make that others can hear infringe as well.

How loudly we walk,
How we chew our food,
How loudly we sneeze, burp or fart.

We can easily get others to **laugh (connect)** or **get upset with us (disconnect)** just by how we choose to make our noises heard in this world.

If we choose to **amplify our own voices,** more people will hear them—

Think protests.
Think TED talks.
Think podcasts.
Think music.

Music is another incredible infringer.

It has the power to **connect** or **divide** within seconds. The style of music opens doors or shuts them just by putting it into a category.

Some people won't listen to anything if it's *country*.
Others want nothing to do with *rap* or *hip-hop*.
Others, still, won't listen to anything if it's considered *secular*.

What you choose to play, out loud, gives others a chance to:

> *Nod along,*
> *Sing with you,*
> *Be inspired,*
> *Leave the room,*
> *Look at you differently... or whatever.*

Again, it gives you the opportunity to:
> **connect, divide,** or make no **difference**.

DeeJay's know this all too well and learn to ***"play to the crowd"*** for this purpose.

And, certainly, music can also connect or disconnect people just by how *loud* it is.

If it's too loud, it's really bothersome to some people.
Others don't enjoy it unless it drowns out everything around them.
If the **bass** is too strong, some people can't stand it and get upset.

It just is.

When we sit at home and do nothing, we don't infringe on anyone or anything—**we just exist.**

However, the minute we go out into public or can be seen or heard or smelled in some fashion, **it's game on**.

You see, we have to be **cognizant of our surroundings** while **finding our own joys**.

They have to play well together.

If the people around you hate something about you and you just can't *"be yourself,"* find different people to hang with.

Life's too short.

If others aren't willing to accept you for you *(that's the response part of the infringement that I didn't touch on),* either make subtle changes that appease others in the short-run *(think not dressing a certain way at a family dinner so as to not rock the boat)* or accept what comes with choosing **not to care** what they're *offended* by.

We all have some things we can control in our own lives—and what I mention here is a mere subset of those things. Each one, as it's exposed to others, comes with a potential to **connect, be neutral**, or **disconnect**. Again, it just is.

And, if life's a dance, let's look at it this way.

We all get to choose **how we dance** throughout our lives and **who gets to watch** to some extent. We don't get to choose whether those that watch will like it, but we do get to choose some of what influences their decisions. We should learn to dance the dances we want to dance and sit out the others.

No matter how much we like our own dancing, someone will always dislike it. *Others won't even know we're dancing.*

Dance with those you want to and *listen to the music that brings you life,* but *don't force it on others.*

Wear what you want and wear it with pride, but don't make others accept your choices—just know that they get to choose based on what you show. Let others dance their dance and enjoy the differences.

Be *cognizant* of the fact that the more you care about *whatever dance you're dancing*, the more you'll *connect* and *divide* your audience.

Dance anyway.

Last, I'll say this.

Being sensitive is merely the awareness of senses.
The more we're aware as leaders, the easier it is to understand how we can influence our own lives by choosing across a wide spectrum of topics and deciding whether we want to **connect, disconnect** *or simply,* **be neutral**. *This works for us as well as our people* **AND** *the organizations we lead.*

Make sense?

SECRET #33

The secret revealed for leaders is that every choice we make, from what we wear to what we say, has the potential to connect, be neutral, or disconnect us from others based on the infringement of their senses—sight, smell, taste, touch, and hearing. Awareness of these influences allows us to navigate life's dance, choosing our steps and understanding that how we present ourselves can either foster connections or create divisions.

34

AFTER THE SONG

What would it look like if leaders **took the lead** in relationship building?

You, me, them—that group over there. We're the leaders I'm talking about. We're the ones that can change this. Not those guys sitting over there in the corner. Or those in the hallway.

Us. The ones that are here and paying attention.

You see, there was a time when genuine connections were built on mutual respect and trust. Relationships formed over time.

People got to **truly know one another** and they forged deep, meaningful friendships. And they valued each other. They spent time on those relationships. They opened up and engaged in conversation.

They asked questions and listened.
They told stories and they laughed.
They shared information and helped each other.
They invited people into their lives and enjoyed their company.

Not everything was calculated—
People either liked you for who you were or they didn't.

There were exceptions, sure, but people were the real deal. They were themselves. Authentic, if you will. They weren't trying to get something out of you.

And that's where I'm going with this.

Years ago, I was standing with a friend at a drink rail that overlooked a large dance floor.

This particular night, I just wanted to enjoy some conversation, have a few drinks, and watch people.

A lady, probably fifteen years my elder had walked over and joined in on the conversation. She's a lady I'd talked to and danced with a number of times in the past as I once taught two-step lessons at that very club.

After about twenty minutes or so a song came on that got her excited and she asked if I'd like to dance. I politely declined—told her I was just there to watch and hang out that night and asked if we could do it the next time when I was there to dance.

By the time the song ended she said, with a bit of a nasty tone, *"Well, there's no reason for me to stay and talk if you're not going to dance,"* and she walked off.

If we'd have been playing poker, she would have just shown her cards before the betting was over—if you catch my drift?

The feeling I was left with was that I only mattered to her for that one thing:

My friendship didn't matter.
The conversation didn't matter.
Getting to know me or my friend didn't matter.

She wanted what she wanted and when she didn't get it, she moved on.

And that was that—I never saw her again.

That moment taught me a lot.

It stung, but it made me realize how many relationships are built on foundations of sand—where one of the two parties is merely looking for a particular thing.

> *A way to "get ahead."*
> *Access to something.*
> *Favoritism or special treatment.*
> *A way to use someone in a manipulative manner to get something out of them.*

And, let's be clear—the reasons why people do this are many.
It's basically that they see something someone else has that's valuable, and they want it. Could be money, property, skills, good looks, power, connections, or even influence.

As leaders, we have to be careful of people who want to take short-cuts—people who come into our lives and make it seem like they're interested in us to get that *thing,* whatever the *thing* is.

But, we also have to look at this as an opportunity—

> *An opportunity to do better.*
> *To be mindful of our own relationships.*
> *To look at ways of contributing to others' lives and adding value.*
> *To not just look to "take" from others.*
> *To not just look at people as one-dimensional.*
> *To watch and be there when people grow, change, and become new versions of themselves.*
> *To respect where they came from, and to accept where they're going.*

To actually build something that will stand the test of time.

And for context, the *"test of time"* is really after the *"song"* ends.
A *"song"* could be a period of time in your life, a job, a project, or a particular moment.

Like, when you're no longer their *leader.*
When you no longer do business with them.
When you no longer have to work with them.
When you're no longer their coach or teacher.
When you no longer have money, property, or the ability to help them in the way that you once could.
When you're no longer able to get them in... for free.

Because, *that* moment—*when the proverbial song ends*—is when you know, for sure, what you've built.

And that's the kind of stuff real leaders build—

> *Relationships with foundations that weather storms.*
> *Relationships that bounce in and out of changes in life—*
> > *good, bad, or indifferent.*
> *Relationships that mutually value each other.*

So, leaders, take the lead...

Get to know people. All people—not just those you lead.
Communicate openly and transparently. Build for the long-term.
Encourage continuous learning. Celebrate successes of others.
Show empathy, use active listening, and be supportive.
Be patient. Talk to them after the *"song"* ends.

Relationships matter.
Don't play the game of just trying to get something out of someone and throwing them to the curb afterwards.

**You're better than that. We don't do that to people.
Not today. Not ever.**

No one deserves to be treated like that.

That said, keep in mind that—

> *Some people aren't interested in building something with you.*
> *Some people don't want to be your friend.*
> *Some people don't want a relationship.*
> *Some people are only interested in getting something out of you.*
> *Some people will throw YOU to the curb the moment their business with you ends—you know, after the song.*

As a leader, it's important to know people like this exist—*and for you to keep your eyes open so you can see the moment they show their cards.*

Leaders with integrity, character, and authenticity know how important these values are.

As such, they look for others with these qualities as well.

Be that kind of leader.

Hold yourself and others accountable to a higher standard.

Be intentional when you build relationships, and pay attention to the little things to ensure it's built on a solid foundation.

Treat others like they matter—
And your relationships will stand for themselves.

And, regardless of what song is playing in your life... when it ends, **don't walk out on people.**

With any luck, the next song will become your favorite—
And you're going to need someone to dance with.

SECRET #34

Leadership is about more than just guiding others; it's about building meaningful relationships based on trust and mutual respect. Take the lead in relationship building by getting to know people on a personal level, communicating openly and transparently, and prioritizing long-term connections over short-term gains. Show empathy, celebrate others' successes, and be patient, even when the "song" ends. Real leaders build relationships with solid foundations that withstand the test of time.

35

GRADING ON A CURVE

What would life be like if we were graded on a curve?

Would the room where we painted three of the four walls yesterday suddenly be complete?

Would we cut half our yard only to see that all of our neighbors only cut half of theirs yesterday—and today we all have a freshly mown lawn with no further effort?

Would we take our driver's test, fail it, and then get a new license sent to us in the mail just because the instructor felt they didn't prepare us for the material?

 The thing is, rarely is ANYTHING graded on a curve in the "real-world." So, why is it acceptable in educational settings?

The answer to this question can—*and often does*—go in many different directions.

> *It could be lack of preparation.*
> *A poorly worded set of questions.*
> *A realization that the material was not taught very well.*
> *A requirement for the entire class to meet a standard.*
> *A bonus or incentive for higher test scores.*

A way to pass the class and move them on to someone else—the
  "not my problem" mentality.
A lack of time to adequately discuss and absorb the material.

I mean, really, the possibilities for *"why"* are seemingly endless.

But does it ultimately help?

So, first, let's look at grades in school. **Are they important?**
Unfortunately, yes:

> *It's an "objective measurement of one's performance" made from*
> *hundreds of "subjective measurements of one's performance."*

In other words—*YES,* it's looked at because it's easy to see...
NOT because it's a reflection of anything to do with knowledge.

Leaders, it's important you understand this next part so you evaluate
the *right things* with your teams.

Okay, back to school again...

Can you get an A and have no idea what you're doing in class? Sure.
Can you get a D and that class change your life? *Emphatically,* **YES!**
Can you get all C's and expect to get into a prestigious college
because you know the material better than anyone? *No—*
And that's the point.

Do students **LOVE IT** when they get graded on a curve? Of course.
And it makes the teacher more likable.

Grades are a game—
And you have to know how to play.

Playing the game, though, isn't really about grades—
Nor is about learning.

It's about meeting or exceeding expectations of those you're working with.

Each teacher is your "boss"—
And each one is temporary.

You may have only one boss or upwards of six or seven at a time and each one has their own set of rules they play by:

> *Some are sticklers for timeliness.*
> *Some are really hard on punctuation.*
> *Some expect eyes on them at all times.*
> *Some like and reward participation in class.*
> *Some demand all thought processes are shown (you know, "show your work") and grade you accordingly.*

Learning what each "boss" values is important.

Knowing what set of rules you're being graded on is critical—not just in a classroom, but in real life.

Playing by *these* rules will help anyone, academically—but really, it's a matter of understanding that it's nothing more than working with different people, or **bosses.**

When *bosses* grade on a curve, **everyone loses.**

It's not *just a grade*—it's an opportunity to *make changes and get better,* **as long as the boss gives you that chance.**

If it's that the class didn't, you know, *get it...*
Is there another way to present the material?

If everyone fails the test...
Can it be revisited so everyone gets a chance to do better after a new type of lesson?

If the curve happens just for the grade—much is lost.

Everyone gets a pass without actually earning it and the long-term impact of that kind of thinking **degrades society over time.**

Things don't just miraculously get better.
Situations don't normally fix themselves.
Yards don't just get cut overnight.
Walls don't just get painted for you.

Someone, somewhere, has to take up the slack.

Best if we teach those who are involved how to play the game better and be responsible for their actions all the way through—

> *Show them that if they make mistakes, there are ways of fixing them in most cases.*
> *Show them that making mistakes or not knowing sometimes is unfixable.*
> *Show them that resourcefulness and understanding is always better than just knowing an answer.*

Ignorance isn't always bliss.
Nor is it always the student's fault.
Both sides should be constantly evaluated.

Students: *Don't look for, ask for, or expect a curve.*

Teachers: *Find new ways to teach, grade, assess, or reinforce material in a way your students "learn"* **WITHOUT** *a curve.*

It's certainly harder, but better for everyone in the long-run.

I mean, if it's *"not important"* they get it—why is it being taught?

I'll take a bad grade any day of the year if it makes me rethink the *"why"* over being graded on a curve and foolishly thinking I deserved it.

Clearly, if I didn't *"make the grade,"* I missed something of importance in the lesson, somewhere.

Don't overlook the opportunities that come with bad grades.

Sometimes, it's the little things that end up mattering—
Or the fine print you missed.

One day, those little things you learned to pay attention to just might become the reason you get to do the big things.

SECRET #35

The secret revealed is that relying on a curve for grading in educational settings doesn't truly help students or promote genuine learning. Grades, in essence, are a game that requires understanding the rules of each "boss" (or teacher), and the focus should be on actual learning and meeting or exceeding expectations, not just on getting a passing grade through a curve.

36

TEAMING UP

Have you ever set up a dating profile?

You look for the best picture you have of yourself.

You write some attention-getting headline with some ego-boosting details about how great you are—and then you give it a whirl and you see what you can attract.

Then, once you see, you adjust.

You change things up. Perhaps a new image. A better headline. More details on some things and less on others. More thought about what you're looking to attract **AND** what you'd like to have in your life.

Ultimately, you're looking to fill a gap in your life with someone you're attracted to.

And, so are they.

Mind you, attraction comes in many flavors other than just vanilla. Vanilla, in this case, is merely what you see at the surface level—you know, like, gauging attractiveness solely on someone's picture online.

 Judging a book by it's cover, so to say.

Other flavors of attraction could be any one of the following:

It could be someone's mind and spirit that draws you in.
It could be their ideas, thoughts, and opinions that just blow you away in conversation.
It could be their background, hobbies, or maturity that knock your socks off.
It could be money, status, or name that impress you like no other (sad, but true). Or—
It could be their knowledge, excitement, or interest on a particular concept or thing that you just can't get enough of.

I mean, really, at the end of the day you want:

Someone who complements what you do, but brings different skills to the table.
Someone you connect with, but they're their own person and you respect them for what they do.
Someone who is authentic and confident in who they are as a person.
Someone who doesn't need to be checked up on throughout the day and someone you look forward to talking to.
Someone who treats people well and has soft skills.
Someone who is interested in learning, growing and making things better. And, ultimately—
Someone you can rely on and trust.

It's really not that different from hiring.

Doesn't matter if you're a small business, run a huge advertising company, have a staff of contractors, or run a tree service—at some point you'll have to look to **team up** with other people and make decisions on who you work with.

And, when I say "team up," I mean that. **YOU** are part of the team.

As in—**they** have to think all of those wonderful things of you as well.

If you're their boss, or "leader," you have to be someone they **WANT** to work for.

As a leader, you need to be:

> Someone who has the potential to add value to their life.
> A leader they can connect with who treats people well and has soft skills.
> A leader who is authentic and confident in who they are as a person.
> A leader who is interested in learning, growing, and making things better.
> A leader who doesn't need to be checked up on and someone they can look forward to talking to. And, ultimately—
> A leader they can rely on and trust.

See how it works?
It's really not that different from dating.

When you hire someone, look for connection and intent.

> Are they likable and do they want to be here?
> Is this someone I could see being a part of my life, daily?
> And will we be able to do great things together?

Think of it like this—
If you only hire someone because of a skill set and overlook everything else, it's the same as merely having a physical attraction to someone.

It's great, at times—
But then you have to walk and talk with that person.

> And eat with them.
> And shop with them.

And travel with them.

Very quickly you'll realize there's nothing more—
And you start to become distant.

It just kills the connection and makes everyone resentful at the end of the day.

That said, don't just hire people just because they can do a "thing," whatever that "thing" is.

**Hire them because of who they are—
and what you can do, together, once they're on the team.**

Think: *"multi-talented,"* or *"multi-faceted,"* or has a *"wide variety of skills and experiences to draw upon."*

Oh, and about that attractiveness thing—*it goes for you, too.*

> *If you're a big-name company, that's attractive to a lot of people.*
> *Your overall compensation package (money, benefits, training, paid time off, etc.) might be a major attractant.*
> *Where someone will work could be part of what attracts them (where the company is located, how much travel there is, or even if it's remote).*
> *And, who you surround yourself with is an attractant (your co-workers; or, if you're still thinking the dating thing, your friends).*

If you rank high on one of these things, but low on the other, the person might not stick around.

Think: *"great work environment, but crap pay."*
Think: *"awesome benefits and location, but a boss that micro-manages and screams a lot."*

They **all** matter—and as a leader, you are responsible for at least some portion of those things.

Now in a small business, you're generally responsible for **ALL** of it.

Will you make mistakes? *Absolutely.*

But, here's the thing—
You'll never have the *right* data available to make the *right* decision.

You have to follow your gut and take chances on people.

You'll know—*right away*—if it's going to work out once you start working with them. And, all of your *preconceived notions* about them will go right out the door—because you'll know.

You'll see it firsthand.
Again, it's just like dating.

Sometimes you get it right on your first try—but not generally.

But, you'll have a pretty good idea if there's at least a chance for a longer-term relationship.

If not—release them and move on... quickly.

So, the more specific you can be with what you're looking for, long-term, the better your chances of finding that kind of person.

The more specific you can be with what you offer, including who you are as a leader (be realistic), the greater your chance of attracting the right person.

 *I'm a firm believer that you can win with a team of average*

players that love working together, enjoy what they do, and are doing their best to get better, daily.

Be the leader your team needs and hire people that—

> *Want to be there,*
> *You like having around, and*
> *Can contribute to what you're building by doing things you don't want to do—or have time to be doing—so they can free you up to keep your business moving forward.*

But it all starts with **you**—being someone **they're attracted to as well.**

SECRET #36

The secret to effective hiring is likened to successful dating, emphasizing the importance of connection and compatibility beyond mere skill sets. Leaders should prioritize qualities such as authenticity, soft skills, and a genuine interest in learning and growth, creating an environment where team members genuinely want to work together. Just as in dating, leaders must recognize the significance of both attraction and intent, ensuring that the team dynamics align with a shared vision for long-term success, ultimately fostering a workplace where everyone contributes and thrives.

37

VICTIM VS. CAPTAIN

Either things happen to you or they happen because of you.

In simple terms, either you play the **VICTIM** or the **CAPTAIN.**

Recently, at our house, I've been hearing a *LOT* about how:

> *"Nothing's fair!" and*
> *"Why's it always me?" and*
> *"Everyone's always against me!"*

It's incessant.

Well, the other day, one of our conversations went deeper as I was talking about having a *"Victim Mentality"* versus a *"Captain Mentality."*

And, it's an interesting thought process that's worth explaining, so here it is—*for you.*

Some people can't seem to catch a break.

They spend all their time and energy playing defense and they tell themselves, regularly, how everything bad happens to them—
And they share this as their go-to narrative.

> *"Why do bad things always happen to ME?"* or

"Why am I the only one that gets caught?" or
"I ALWAYS have the worst luck!"

Sound familiar?
Perhaps you've even said one of these on occasion?
We probably all have.

Well, here's the thing.

Life's not fair—and bad things happen to everyone.
No one's exempt.
Not you. Not me.

And, sometimes, bad luck is just that—bad luck.
Truly being in the wrong place at the wrong time.

It happens. But there's more to it.

Luck—good or bad, is temporary.
It's when a **recurring theme** happens that eyebrows start to get raised.

You see:

> *"Bad luck" is often a result of poor choices or bad decisions.*
>   *—Not always.*
> *"Good luck" is often a result of good choices or good decisions.*
>   *—Again, not always.*

Everyone is a victim at some point as a result of being harmed, injured or assaulted in a crime, accident or an event—*heck, even verbally from a friend or family member.*

Being betrayed, lied to or taken advantage of falls into this realm as well—and they happen to all of us.

Now, to be clear, I'm not making light of **being a victim**.

When you're a victim of something, heck even a *victim of circumstance,* you have to isolate it and do your best to deal with that *circumstance* independently.

It's a big deal, and you have to work through the pain.

Please understand though, where I'm going with this **ISN'T** about isolated incidents. You'll see.

Can you have *"good luck"* when gambling or playing the lottery? Sure. But that's not what this is about either.

A **Victim Mentality** or mindset (we'll call it a professional victim) is different. This is not an isolated event—but rather, it's an ongoing narrative that says: *"I have no control over what happens to me."*

It's a sense of **powerlessness** over situations—where you feel like you can't change anything about what happens to you.

And, every time something happens **TO** them, it confirms their belief that **EVERYTHING BAD** happens **ONLY** to **THEM**.

It's a very self-centered and narrow-minded approach to life.

And, it's exhausting—both for that person who's just waiting for the next bad thing to happen to them, as well as those that have to listen to them spew the negativity.

The Victim Mentality, though, is not a permanent thing, and can be changed at any point:

> *Sometimes it's a matter of walking away.*
> *Sometimes it's a matter of running.*

*Sometimes it's a matter of dropping communications with
  loved ones.*
Sometimes it's a matter of quitting a job.
Sometimes it's a matter of filing for divorce or breaking things off.
Sometimes it's a matter of moving away.
Sometimes it's a matter of calling authorities.

STOP putting yourself in the same situation day after day.
And, *STOP* the foolishness of provoking someone else to the point that they take an action that makes you feel like a victim again.

Some people just bring out the worst in us—and we have to learn to manage our interactions better.

Not having these interactions IS a form of 'managing.'

The point is, rarely will your situation be permanent unless **YOU** let it be. Most things in life are temporary—and you have to be willing to move, or take an action for things to be different.

 **The moment you start taking actions, you put on your captain's hat.**

Be careful though—
Not everyone will appreciate your new hat.

Resistance. Hatred. Lashing out.

There will be others who will try to hold you back. Others who like or prefer the old you as it benefited them in some way.

This is about **YOU**, though, **not them**.

What you get when you change your mindset is **SO** much better.

A sense of pride and self-worth will join forces with you and you start taking control over your situation because you are, after all, the boss. The leader. The captain.

THIS is YOUR ship.

So, wait! What's the *Captain's Mentality?*
No, it's not the feeling you get after too much spiced rum.
Well, it kinda is, but that's different.

> The **Captain Mentality** I'm talking about is a frame of mind that things will happen **BECAUSE** of you, not just to you.

Good and bad can happen, but the captain gets to set the course of the navigation.

That's what leadership is about.

Being your own captain says:

> *You're able to make decisions and that you can react accordingly.*
> *You can change your situation.*
> *You can change your mind.*
> *You can influence decisions around you.*
> *You can make expectations known.*
> *You can clearly set boundaries.*
> *You can choose who you talk to and who you listen to.*
> *You can stand up for yourself or others in need.*
> *You can be an advocate or a catalyst for change.*

*If your life was a book—**and it is**—being the captain allows YOU to write your own story instead of letting others write it for you.*

Don't just play the passive role and think it'll all just work itself out.

Statements like:

> "It's just not meant to be," or
> "God's in control," or
> "If it's God's will..." or
> "Give it to God," and
> "It's what God has in store for your life."

Those are great and all, but they leave **YOU** out as a variable—
And powerless.

Now, if those thoughts struck a nerve with you, pay attention to this next part:

Everything about having a *Captain's Mentality* revolves around **taking an active role** in one's life. If you believe in God, then this is where He would be your **co-captain** (you might be more familiar with the term *copilot*).

Again, this implies action—as in:
Do something... Right or wrong, do something.

As your own captain, things happen *because of you*—
Not always good.
Not always bad.
But definitely as a result of **YOU** being involved.

No longer should you be blaming anyone else.
It's about being responsible.

This is where you think:

> "What could I have done different to prevent this?" or
> "What can I do better next time?"

And last—
Understand that everyone out there is doing something similar.

We don't always have **control** over our situations at a **macro level** (environment, politics, or whatever), but most of the time we have tons of choices on a **micro level** (our daily lives)—and **THAT's** what this is about.

Being a victim is different than having a victim's mindset.
Know and understand the difference.

Being your own captain is about having the *freedom to choose* your destinations.

It also means you might just sink your own ship if you're not paying attention.

Victim's Mentality or **Captain's Mentality**?

Your choice doesn't just affect you—
It affects everyone around you.

Choose wisely.

SECRET #37

The secret revealed is that life presents two roles: the victim, where things happen to you, or the captain, where things happen because of you. Embracing a Captain's Mentality involves taking an active role, making choices, and accepting responsibility for one's life; steering the ship of destiny with awareness and purpose.

38

BATTERIES

Everyone who owns an EV knows how critical it is to keep its battery charged.

Depending on what you drive, the size of your battery, and the size of your charging port, a charge could take anywhere from thirty minutes to twelve hours.

Is it always convenient? *No.*
Is it readily available on every corner? *Also no.*
Do you need to set aside time in your off time to make sure to do it? **Yes.**

It's the same for leaders.

Your battery needs to be recharged, and running it to zero can have detrimental effects.

You have to be mindful of the kinds of things that drain your battery and those that help recharge it—and you have to be intentional.

And, it's not the same for everyone.

This is about **self-awareness,** and something you really need to know about yourself.

So, first, what drains your battery?

For some, it's managing diverse personalities, resolving interpersonal conflicts, or fostering collaboration.

Or, maybe it's the stress that comes with uncertainty and making decisions without complete information.

Perhaps it's high expectations of you or your team, or lack of recognition from those around or above you.

For me, the three biggies are:

> Dealing with incompetence,
> Working with people who simply don't care about others or their work, and
> Having to interface with people who say one thing and do another.

Just like EVs, the size of our batteries—*and what drains them—*
Is different for everyone.

 *But, more importantly:* **What recharges your battery?**

As in, **what re-energizes you,** as a leader?

What kinds of things can you do that allow you to fill your battery up near capacity so you can *bring it* when you return to your team?

Again, this is different for everyone.
And you need to know **what works,** and **what doesn't.**

Unlike cars that need to be plugged in, one of the most important factors for leaders is to **unplug.**

Unplugging means **creating boundaries** between work and personal life. Unplugging allows you to **rejuvenate mentally and emotionally.**

Things that may help you recharge include:

> *Exercise,*
> *Reading for pleasure, or*
> *Nature retreats.*
> *Quality time(s) with loved ones is big, too, as long as they're not also a drain.*

You may enjoy:
> *Journaling,* dancing, or traveling for exploration.

Perhaps you're into:
> *Yoga, meditation, or even reading the Bible.*

For me, this one's easy as I have several go-to's—sports is my favorite.

Actively playing or being involved in some kind of *sport* disengages the world around me: golf, baseball, football, tennis, basketball, dancing, racketball, playing catch, fishing—*doesn't matter, they all re-energize me.*

Other things that fill my battery include anything to do with coaching *(sports, dance, business, school),* large social gatherings, and deep conversations over coffee or at a pub.

Whatever gets you to unplug and reconnect with yourself is in play. And, if you don't have something that recharges you—find something.

When your battery is low, it can end up having detrimental effects on: productivity, your immune system, and relationships, in general.

We all have to be mindful of our batteries—
How they affect us, and how they affect others.

And, as leaders, it's important to take care of ourselves *AND make sure those that follow us are taking care of theirs.*

That said, now's a good time to take inventory of yourself—

What's the life of your battery?
What kinds of things drain your battery?
And, what do you do for yourself that re-energizes YOU?

And, be honest—
*If your life is full of things that drain you, now's the time to make a change. A battery that is **depleted**, regularly, is really difficult to charge.*

So, let's make this simple.

All batteries matter. As a leader, you're going to need yours ***charged up AND*** you'll need to be ready to help ***jump-start someone else's.***

Else, a leader can't lead and a follower can't follow.

We're all in this together.

SECRET #38

The secret lies in recognizing the importance of recharging one's own "battery," understanding what drains it, and intentionally engaging in activities that re-energize. Just as electric vehicles require charging, leaders need to unplug and create boundaries between work and personal life to mentally and emotionally rejuvenate. By taking inventory of personal batteries, identifying drains, and prioritizing activities that bring energy, leaders not only enhance their own well-being but also contribute to building a resilient and energized team.

39

MUST BE PRESENT TO WIN

Must be present to win.

How many times have you heard this in your life?

A raffle. A sweepstakes. An award ceremony. A company-wide celebration. A radio-station gimmick. Giveaways. Entry into this, that, or the other?

But—what if it's one of those little life secrets?

One that has much more to do with **relationships, family dynamics, friendships, happiness,** AND **leadership.**

One that states the obvious, but is much *deeper* than what you see on the surface.

 *Life isn't about collecting things (shells, cards, money, dolls, etc.,) it's about* **experiences, consciousness, connections—** *and* **being present.**

It's less about consuming and filling our minds with entertainment, gossip and political garbage, and more about **showing up** and being a part of something—anything.

Being present is intentional.
It's a choice.

You can't be everywhere at all times and everything to all people, but you can sure ***go deep where it matters.***

> *Being present says you're not on your phone or distracted with a hundred other things when you're with someone.*
> *Being present says you're there supporting someone else.*
> *Being present says you're awake.*
> *Being present says you're in the moment.*
> *Being present says the here and now is important.*
> *Being present says whatever it is you're doing matters.*
> *Being present says you care.*
> *Being present says your priorities are in order.*

And, sure, ***resources matter.***

If you can't afford to support someone's effort, that's okay—
you can still be present in the best way you know how.

If you don't have the time to support someone's effort, that's okay too. You can still be ***present*** by supporting them emotionally or in some other way.

Being present is a mindset as well as a verb.
It takes action.
It takes thought.

Being present is about both ***doing AND being.***

When someone doesn't have time for you—
  You sense it.
When someone doesn't show up for you in the way you expect—
  You notice it.
When someone doesn't support you in the way you need—
  You feel it.

So, perhaps, the best way to counter all those things if you've felt them is to:

  Be the one that's present.
  Be the change.
  Be the light.

Be the one that says,
  "I'm here and ready to win,"
    —without having to say anything at all.

Because, frankly, in the game of life, we can all be winners—
But it's definitely the one game where you ***must be present to win***.

SECRET #39

The secret revealed is that in the game of life, to truly win, one must be present. It emphasizes the importance of intentional presence, showing up, and actively participating in meaningful experiences and connections, as opposed to merely collecting material possessions or being distracted by the superficial aspects of life.

40

SUPER HEROES

grew up in an era where a few main characters were celebrated as those that saved the day.

They were heroes, but not the kind that Hogan had in his show.

They were **super,** as in **larger than life.**
They made things happen.
They gave us hope that one day, when we need them most,
they'd show up and save the world.

Superman was probably my favorite of all them.
Batman was cool, too, but didn't have the same feel for me.
The Incredible Hulk was inspiring in a different way.

All crimefighters, of sorts—
And all showed us who the true **"bad guys"** were.

Or, so we thought.

Then, as I grew up my *heroes* turned more towards *those who fought for or saved the girl.* Inspirations included a bit of pop culture at the time: The Karate Kid, Indiana Jones, Dirty Dancing, Road House, the double-O-seven series.

I used to dream of how I'd one day take a bullet for a girl—
And then we'd live happily ever after.

You know, "manly" stuff.

Somewhere around the same time period in my life I also had real-life *sports heroes* that had fame. Those I thought could do it all.

I went through the phases of following each one and trying to emulate. Whenever I was playing a sport, I was someone else.

In my head I was Michael Jordan with a sweet pass, then Andre Agassi with my racket and Roger Clemens when I pitched.

I was Larry Bird behind the 3-point line, then Mike Tyson with gloves on, and then Hulk Hogan when we wrestled.

I was Jim McMahon with my sweat bands and then I was fist-pumping like Tiger Woods (you couldn't see it right then, but I was just doing the fist pump).

Fast forward a few years and my heroes turned to people who were building businesses and seemed to have it all.

The early days of Amazon, Google, FaceBook, Microsoft, Apple, and even YouTube. It was exciting—and those **characters** now seemed like the people who would save things.

The ones who would transform our world and make it better.

Leaders—they were all leaders in their own right.

Different kinds.
Different flavors.
But leaders.

People followed them.
I was one of those people.

I studied the characters, the athletes, and the ones who ran the businesses.

> *I watched mannerisms.*
> *I watched their attitude.*
> *I watched the way they performed "on stage," regardless of what their "stage" was.*
> *I read up on what they do and how they did it.*

But it was all for show.
And I mean that.
It wasn't their reality, it was just what I was allowed to see.

What they *wanted* me to see.

*It was to **show me possibilities.***
*It was to **show me that I could do anything.***
*It was to **show me different ways of succeeding** and how success could be found in a variety of ways.*

So I used what I learned and added them to my arsenal.
I became my own person through inputs of others.
I built what I could build—both with my business as well as my family.

Then, one day, my little girl told her teacher I was her hero.

Me.

Not someone on TV.
Not someone playing a sport.
Not someone I read about in the newspaper or a magazine.
Not someone building the largest business in the world.

Me.

And that was that—***my perspective had changed.***

 ***From that day forward, I looked at things differently.***
I wanted to see what she saw. I wanted to see and perceive the world around me and not from a telephoto lens.

And, guess what?

Because of her, the **heroes** I see today are far greater than anything I ever saw in a movie.

The athletes I once put on pedestals have all stepped down to make room for the ones I see now.

The heroes I once heralded are not the everyday heroes that have made a difference to me, nor the ones I hear about from others.

The folks I see as heroes, now, don't wear capes.
They don't read scripts.
They're not paid actors.
They're not sponsored by anyone.

They're **leaders of people** and those that are out making a difference.

They don't just talk about things and tell people what to do—
They show up and help get it done.

They say things like:

> *"How can I help?"* or
> *"Where can I jump in?"* or
> *"Let me take this off your plate so you can focus on what matters,"* or
> *"I'll be right over and we'll figure it out together."*

They're everyday folks who have turned into the very characters we all saw growing up.

They're out there in our communities having conversations—
And holding people's hands.

They're showing up and volunteering their time to rebuild houses for those who've lost it all.

They're organizing GoFundMe campaigns for people who've had tragedy strike.

They're paying debts for others just because.

They don't do it for the fame.
They don't do it for the money.
They don't do it because someone else told them to.

And there's more:

> *They're the teachers who connect with the kids no one talks to.*
> *They're the ones who fight battles that aren't theirs.*
> *They're folks who are battling diseases and they just won't give up.*
> *They're people who connect those that can help with those that need it.*
> *And they're the ones getting their hands dirty even though no one asked for help.*

Turns out, I was right all along...

> **Heroes** are, in fact, **Super**—
> As in **Larger Than Life.**

They make things happen. They show up when we need them most, and they save our world—however small our world is.

If you want to be a superhero, you just have to be the kind of leader that truly cares about the well-being of your people...

"Your people" can be defined as those on your team, at home, or in your community. It's those you choose to serve who need someone like you to swoop in and save the day.

Superheroes are real—I've seen them.
And so have you.

Perhaps now's the time for you to suit up and get your cape on?

All you have to do is:

> *Look out for your people,*
> *Find ways to make things happen, and*
> *Show up in a way that matters.*

Up, up, and away!

SECRET #40

The secret to being a superhero lies in everyday leadership—those who make a difference by showing up and getting things done without seeking fame or recognition. They don't wear capes or read scripts; they're ordinary people making an extraordinary impact in their communities. To become a superhero, one just needs to care deeply about the well-being of others, show up when needed, and find ways to make a meaningful difference in the lives of those they serve.

41

STRONG SUPPORT SYSTEM

How important is a strong support system?

Depends, right?

Are we talking about structural support or human support?

Interestingly, they're similar.

Drywall, in and of itself, can provide some basic support.
Any single human, in and of itself, can provide some basic support.

The greater the potential load in either case, the greater the need for something stronger below the surface.

Having the right tools to find, tap into, and use foundational pieces like studs is essential if the potential stress level is high, **else failure is imminent.**

It's not as easy for humans to find, tap into, and use strong foundational pieces *in other humans.*

You can't just buy a tool and scan people's heads *(although that'd be super cool!).*

Ultimately, it'll come from either friends, family or professionals and trusted advisors *(this could include books, online videos, blog posts, spiritual leaders, etc).*

Family members may be able to help you with the type of support you need—**but they might not.**

Friends may be able to help you with the type of support you need—**but they may not.**

Professionals may be able to help you with the type of support you need—**but they may not.**

Each of the *human examples* can provide surface level support at a minimum, but beyond that, you have to develop your own internal tools so you'll know how to get and gauge the right type of human support for what you're going through or need help with.

I say human support because it's different than faith-based support.

 ***The statement, "No man is an island!" essentially says we'd all fail miserably if we were completely on our own.***

As a leader, who can you *really* turn to and trust in a time of need? Who do you *physically* go to for support?

The song, ***"Lean on me!"*** is a great example of how we all need someone to lean on. I'll be there for you and help you—and before long I'll need someone too.

Think: support—
In the form of human connection.

Ultimately, no one can do it all without support.

It's impossible.

And you'll need lots of support and, generally, it'll come from a combination of all three sources.

Support from only one of the three (family, friends, or professionals) will often create its own stress over time.

Look for options of who to go to in a time of need.
Maybe tap more than one of your support groups?

Varied views and perspectives help you build your own foundation—and the stronger it is, the more weight you can withstand.

The stronger your own foundation, the easier it is to help others by sharing **YOUR** experiences.

And, it's important to **give** support as well as **receive.**

Don't just take from others as that's a short-term one-sided strategy that doesn't end well long-term.

And, beware of those who merely use you for yours without any reciprocation. It'll drain you.

Look for support—

> *Go beyond surface levels.*
> *Help others.*
> *Lean and be leaned on.*

Strong foundational support systems are essential for each of us to thrive—especially, leaders.

SECRET #41

The secret revealed is that a strong support system, whether in structural or human form, is crucial for facing life's challenges. It emphasizes the need for a well-developed internal toolkit to identify and utilize various sources of support—family, friends, and professionals—to build a robust foundation for personal growth and mutual assistance.

42

MIND YOUR BUSINESS

It's likely you've heard or used the phrase, *"Mind your business."* And, in certain circumstances, it's probably warranted.

Like, for example, the time I was in a large executive meeting that was about to begin and I asked a senior engineer why his pinky nail was way longer than any of his others.

Mm-hmm.
Yep, that's one moment I'd like to take back.

That said, let's use this phrase in a whole new way.
Some new context, if you will.

Let's make it something positive to say to someone instead of it being used the way we've always used it.

To simplify, we're giving an old phrase a new meaning and turning *"mind your business"* into positive actions we can all take.

*From a leadership perspective, it's about harnessing the power of your mind to unleash unique successes for you **AND** those you're leading.*

Let's start by breaking the phrase down.
Three words. ***Mind, Your,*** and ***Business.***

The **mind** portion deals with what's *"inside your head,"* not what you can glean using the latest AI tools (more on those at the end).

The **your** portion is that it's for you to do—as in, take action.

And the **business** part is whatever it is you do where you can utilize the resources we're about to cover.

 **And, since the "mind" part is, by far, the most important, it'll be the main focus of this chapter.**

Here goes—

As leaders, we all need a toolkit.
One that has drawers and keeps tools for our mind—
You know, to help us work smarter, not harder.

Think of each drawer as a different set of tools.

I recommend a toolkit that has at least three drawers to start, but **one** that's scalable.

Here's what your three drawers will contain:

>*The first drawer houses **mental models**.*
>*The second, **visualization techniques**.*
>*The third, **mindfulness**.*

What tools are in them? Let's explore.

We'll look at mental models first as there are many worth knowing.

The more you know, the quicker you enhance your critical-thinking skills as well as your decision-making.

In other words, don't overlook the importance here.

The first mental model to learn is **Systems Thinking.**

It's a deep-dive in and of itself, but a must for your drawer as it allows you to zoom out and see a much larger set of variables when looking at problems.

Understanding **Confirmation Bias** is another to know as it's critical to ensure assumptions are being challenged and not just stacked because we were looking for them.

The Pareto Principle is another that helps leaders prioritize efforts and focus on the most impactful ones. That one's also called the **80-20 rule** and it's worth exploring.

There are several others, but here's a few worth noting:

Cost-Benefit Analysis—this one helps when it comes to weighing trade-offs and making informed choices.

SWOT Analysis—this one's a must for leaders as you'll want to at least know what it's good for, how to build it out, what to look for—and why.

And, of course, you should understand the different mental models of leadership so you'll know when and how to use them. These include:

Transformational *leadership,*
Servant *leadership, and*
Situational *leadership.*

The second major drawer of your toolkit contains **visualization techniques.**

Visualization techniques can be as simple as imagining yourself in some future role after doing whatever it is you're doing.

This is called **Future-Self Visualization** and it allows you to see yourself differently than you currently are.

Outcome Visualization is similar, but it's based on you imagining the positive impact your actions will have on individuals, teams, and the organization as a whole. **Goal Visualization** is similar in its structure.

A **Vision Board** is another useful tool in that you get to see whatever it is you put on it—could be images, quotes, symbols, signs, or whatever works to help inspire and align *good feelings* with the future you envision.

Mental Rehearsal is another technique that's commonly used and it's a great way to practice upcoming situations, to think through objections, to work through responses, and to rev up your confidence in yourself as you'll have a pretty good idea as to what to expect.

Mindfulness is the third drawer and it's worth filling up.

Mindfulness helps leaders cultivate self-awareness, manage stress, and enhance overall effectiveness.

Being **mindful** *is its own super power and can be generated several ways:*

> *Mindful breathing,*
> *Mindful walking,*
> *Mindful listening,*
> *Mindful eating, and*
> *Mindful pauses.*

Each one allows you to disengage, momentarily, and focus on some specific **"thing."**

If, for example, you focus on **breathing—**
Then you'd close your eyes, inhale deeply through your nose, exhale slowly through your mouth and you'd focus on the sensations felt as your breath enters and exits your body.

If it's **walking—**
You'd key in on the sensations of each step as you walk, what part of the foot you use, how you swing your arms, how your hands flow, if your knees are flexed, how much tilt you have at the waist, and what the environment you're in looks and sounds like.

Your toolkit will consist of several **mind resources** developed over time, and they're worth developing.

And yes, there are other models, techniques, grids, and theories that can be used—as a matter of fact, **you should use AI to assist you** by providing more tools and guidance for what you do *specifically*, but it's up to you to take the action to learn and implement them.

In other words, **don't rely on AI to be your mind—**instead, use it as a resource to help **YOU** fill each drawer of **YOUR** toolkit.

Think of AI as a really smart, but lazy friend.
One that has all the right answers to advise you, but won't actually lift a finger to help with anything.

The more you **"mind your business,"** the greater your chance of having success with whatever you do.

And, by all means, teach others to mind their business, especially if they work with you as this will help create a culture of collaboration, balance, creativity, and effectiveness as people rely on other *people—* and not just automated tools.

Your mind is your greatest asset—
And you should continuously develop it to help prepare for tomorrow and tomorrow's tomorrow.

MIND your business—

And you'll very quickly become the leader others look up to,
but *not because you kept to yourself.*

SECRET #42

The secret revealed is that "minding your business" in leadership isn't just about staying out of other people's affairs; it's about harnessing the power of your mind to enhance your effectiveness and success. By filling your toolkit with mental models, visualization techniques, and mindfulness practices, you equip yourself with the resources needed to navigate complex challenges and drive positive outcomes. So, instead of simply focusing on external factors, prioritize the development of your mind as your greatest asset and watch as you become the leader others admire and respect.

43

POWER OUTAGES

Do you know what the purest form of leadership is?

It's when someone—*who's not in charge*—gets others to follow them.

It's the moment others choose to follow someone's lead because they *want to—not have to.*

And, no, it's not because of someone's title.
It's not because of their degree.
It's not because they run the place.
It's not because they're the coach.

It's because they have a story worth listening to.
Or, skills that are worth noting.
Or, knowledge that's worth knowing.
Or, it's because they've been there and done that.
Or, sometimes it's just an air of confidence.

It's called leading without power.

Or, as the title suggests, when there's a **Power Outage**—not literally, but when there's a lack of formal power structure that tells others who's *supposed* to be in charge.

This can happen at work with a co-worker, peer, or subordinate.
It can happen in a school project with an impromptu team of five.
It can happen when working on a project at home with a spouse, a neighbor, or a friend.
It can happen at church or on a field.

Someone steps up and takes the lead.

They become the light. Their own **power source.**
They take responsibility for the *"thing,"* whatever the *"thing"* is.

It's almost always informal, but it allows for a quick structure to form and, almost always, it results in a single person **leading,** and others **following.**

We all find ourselves in these types of situations throughout our lives. Sometimes it just happens, but once you understand how it works, you'll find yourself stepping up more and more.

Think about these next three points the next time you have the chance to lead when *"the power's out."*
Meaning, when there's no formal authority.

First, can you be trusted *to lead whatever it is you're stepping into?*
Do you know something about it and should others follow your lead?
Do you have some form of expertise or credibility that others don't have?

Second, are you a good communicator?
Can you express your ideas clearly, actively listen, and adapt your communication style to meet the personalities you're working with? Not just, in general, but about whatever it is you're trying to take the lead on.

In other words, can you shed *light* on the subject?

Third (*and this one has to happen as you begin*),
Is there a common goal?
Is it clear what everyone is working towards?
Is the objective shared and is there buy-in from everyone involved?

Leading, in general, **requires skills** that don't just pop up out of no-where, but that matter.

Like:

> *Caring about those you lead.*
> *Picking up on emotional cues from others and adjusting.*
> *Being flexible enough to try new things while still steering the ship towards the shared goal.*
> *Being okay with not having to always be right and providing a solid example relating to work ethic, commitment, and your values.*

When the power's out, people follow those that are worth following.

Doesn't matter if there's a title, formal authority, or some hierarchy that tells them anything about you, they'll know—just by watching and listening.

If you want to become the best leader you can be in a formal setting, start with learning to lead people **when they don't have to follow you.**

And, if you get really good at leading without power, you've taken a major step towards becoming **a leader worth following.**

SECRET #43

The secret to leadership lies in its purest form—when someone, regardless of formal authority, inspires others to follow based on trust, expertise, or an air of confidence. It transcends titles or degrees and occurs when individuals take responsibility for a task, displaying good communication skills and fostering a shared goal. Becoming an effective leader, both formally and informally, involves caring for those you lead, adapting to emotional cues, and setting a positive example of work ethic and values.

44

MEASURING YOUR WORTH

How do you measure your worth?

How do you measure others' worth?

*I measure mine based on **impact**. As in:*

> *Am I positively impacting others' lives in some form or fashion?*
> *Am I setting examples others can follow?*
> *Am I learning, growing, and giving back in a way others can benefit?*
> *Am I asking thoughtful questions?*
> *Am I upfront and real with people?*
> *Am I dependable?*
> *Do I listen to others? As in, actively listen, and try to learn who they really are and what they really think?*
> *Am I the kind of friend I'd like to have?*
> *Do I treat people well regardless of their age, job, car, money, political views, religious views, etc.?*

I have never measured my worth by money or material things, and yet I constantly see and hear people talk about how much money this person has, how many followers that person has, who's a part of what church, how many likes some celebrity got, or why we should listen to any political figure just because.

It's rampant here in a small town.
It's probably like that where you are as well.

I wish more people would measure others by **who they really are—
And not by their stuff, status, role or by money.**

We'd have a completely different set of people leading the way.

And, I think more emphasis would go into **leading,**
what it takes to lead,
and what responsibilities are associated.

*Now, if you're measuring others' worth by something tangible or by a title,
what are you really measuring?*

If they lose it all, do they become worthless to you?

Think about it—if you remove the tangible parts of what you know about people, how would you measure their worth?
Would it change?
Would you really put up with the nonsense or rudeness or guilt trips?
Would you change how you spend your time and who you hang with?

What if it's family?
Same kind of deal.

*It's interesting to think like this because it makes you think in a way that's not the **norm** in today's day and age.*

It allows you focus less on pursuing material possessions and more on doing right for yourself and by others.

And, maybe, you'd seek out higher quality people to spend your time with.

And please don't misunderstand: **higher quality** isn't in a degree, a title, a car, a house, or even in a building—
It's **internal**.

And those people are everywhere—you just have to find them.

Value, or worth, is **subjective**, so your definition will probably be different than mine though we'll have some overlaps.

But, it allows you to look beyond the surface and get to really know people.

Do me a favor and spend a few minutes thinking about how you measure your own worth—and what you measure about others.

If, all of a sudden, you had nothing, how would people treat you?

> *How would you treat others if all their possessions or status went away?*
> *How would you treat your friends if they no longer went to your church or bought from your store?*

More so, if you think about yourself...

> *Would people like you more if you bought that new widget?*
> *Would they respect you more if you got a promotion or if you got a new job?*
> *What if you drove a nicer car?*
> *What if you dated or married that one person?*

What if you were the boss and hired a bunch of your friends and paid them well? I'll bet you'd become super popular with them... in front of you.

Now, try having layoffs and see if they treat you any differently.

And, let's take it to the extreme—

> *Do you think people would treat you any differently if you won the lottery?*

Man oh man, I wouldn't wish that on anyone.
The level of fake friends would be unfathomable.

There's no right answer.
There's just right for you and **YOU** get to set your threshold.

Set it high.
Just don't set it on something that can be seen or that can disappear.

And, the thing is, we all have some **biases.**
We all *judge books by covers.*

We all, to some extent, judge others on what we see or hear about them as it allows us to quickly assess, without much thought, whether or not we should trust that person.

Problem is, what we see is not what we get.
It's just a hard lesson to learn.

Get real.
Go deep.
Invest in yourself and your friends.
Watch and learn.
And then make the call on what their worth is.

As leaders, we have to understand what's really important about people—and it's not what most people think.

Leave money or status or things in and your decision is clouded.

Think deeply on this one and start your own conversation with friends, family, and co-workers:

How do you measure your worth?
How do you measure the worth of others?

Think about it.

SECRET #44

The secret revealed is that true worth is not measured by tangible possessions, titles, or external factors, but by the impact one has on others, the quality of the relationships, and the internal qualities that define character. This chapter encourages self-reflection on how one evaluates their own worth and challenges you to look beyond superficial measures when assessing the value of others.

45

WINNERS

All of it.
Every single minute.

If given the choice, that's how much of my time I would spend with winners.

Oh, don't get get me wrong.
These people aren't necessarily the ones winning at things.

Wait... what?

You see...
Winning happens at a single event.
Being a winner is a mindset.

You can lose at an event and still be a winner.

How so?

Winning is largely due to who your competitors are, as well as many factors outside a players control *(the other team gets sick, disqualifications, bad luck, rules violations, better competitors not showing up, cheating, etc).*

You can **win** *(and many people do)* and **NOT** be a winner.

Conversely, *being a winner* has to do with who you are as a person *AND* your mindset.

How you think, prepare, respond and act are all represented here. How you handle adversity as well as how you handle the spotlight.

> *Winners embrace challenges and look for ways to overcome.*
> *Winners don't blame others for failures or disappointments.*
> *Winners take personal responsibility for their actions.*
> *Winners say yes to grinding and putting in the work when no one is watching.*

People only interested in winning an event will never fully be satisfied —because there's always another event to compete in.

Think about it—when non-winners win, the feelings surrounding the win are often **blasé,** at best.

But... **when winners win,** it's truly exciting as it's often recognized that they **deserved** it.

And, better yet, a person can be a winner in **all aspects** of his or her life—and that's what makes it so attractive.

Being a winner involves **integrity, character, discipline, forward-thinking,** and a **growth mindset** (as well as many other qualities like wanting the best for others).

Winning simply requires a first-place finish and merely showing up (there are plenty of people and teams who have won because they were the only ones in the competition—don't let this trick your brain).

Being a winner is the ***whole package,***
regardless of who or what you're up against.

And, importantly:

Athletics are just one area where winners can be found. They're in every business, industry and profession—and they're also just ordinary people doing their best to raise their family.

So, to me:

NO, winning is **NOT** everything—
But being a winner **IS.**

Winners will find a way to win, with or without a medal or a trophy. Winners get up and try again when they get knocked down.

Being a winner is a **choice,** a **mindset,** an **attitude.**

Showing up is important, but **HOW** you show up is critical.

In other words, ***don't confuse winning with being a winner.***

Leaders, strive to be a version of yourself that allows you to call yourself a **winner,** no matter what.

SECRET #45

The secret revealed is that true success as a leader lies not in winning events, which can be influenced by external factors, but in cultivating a winner's mindset characterized by integrity, discipline, resilience, and a growth mindset. Being a winner is a choice and an attitude that transcends mere victories, emphasizing personal growth, responsibility, and the ability to overcome challenges.

46

TRUST, BUT VERIFY

This is no ordinary golf ball
(you'll envision it momentarily).

It's a reminder.
It's a symbol.
It's a lesson.

It's a treasured ball in our house because it represents **character, integrity**, and **honesty.**

It's not the Nike symbol on it.
It's not the random display of sharpie dots.
It's not a hole-in-one ball or the ball that made some miraculous shot during that one tournament.

It's literally just a ball.

Well, more specifically, it's the ball of a recent competitor—
A girl who won a tournament that two of my girls were playing in.

I know because this particular morning started with an impromptu meeting of players and parents grouped together about twenty minutes before tee-time and we were all talking golf when the young lady pulled out her ball and explained her unique pattern to us and showed us the ball she'd be playing.

She was fun and upbeat and it was a great start to the day.

From there, each of the girls showed their unique balls and everyone was *"in the know"* so there would be no confusion.

Fast forward to the 15th hole.

A drive to the right by one of the girls.
Another to the right.
Another to the right.

And then, a long, errant drive over a small hill and behind some trees off to the left where none of the girls could see it.

From my viewpoint, I noted quickly where the ball came in and, based on its trajectory, about where it would be (something I always do to help locate missing balls).

I helped the girls on the right locate their balls fairly quickly and they prepared their shots.

I then noticed that the girl who hit off to the left had walked about 40 yards farther than where I thought her ball was, and, just as I started to alert her, she stopped and hit her ball.

From where she hit, she had an incredible line to the pin, hit it close and ended up with a birdie.

Good stuff!

All the girls told her how great her shot was and congratulated her while she ate it up.

I watched, smiled, and nodded my head slowly while my mind wandered backwards and wouldn't let me forget what I'd just seen.

I told my wife and other two kids to go ahead and that I'd catch up as I wanted to see something first.

I went over to where I thought her ball should have landed only to see that it was all marked as **out of bounds.**

White lines.
Clear as day.
Interesting.

Where she hit from was in bounds, but not where I thought the ball was.

About forty-five seconds into my search in the approximate area where I thought the ball would be—*it appeared.*

I recognized the exact markings on it.

I looked up and verified it was on the line I thought it was on. It was.

I walked back over and looked to the tee box to verify that there wasn't another group hitting yet. There wasn't.

I then looked around to see if there was another group of people maybe looking for a ball with identical markers. Nope. No one around.

So I picked it up and didn't say anything.

I watched the rest of the round and then watched this girl accept her first place trophy while chuckling and saying how lucky she was as she had played so poorly.

I just smiled and congratulated her.

Why did I not say anything?

> *It wasn't my daughter who did this (if it had been, she most likely would have been disqualified).*
> *Parents aren't allowed to call rules infractions on other players.*
> *There was very little at stake and I chose to use it as a lesson for the future instead of right then.*
> *It would have been extremely uncomfortable for her, for her parents, and for everyone involved.*
> *I could have been wrong (I seriously doubt it, but I could have been).*

So... That night, at dinner, I pulled out the ball and said,

> *"Does anyone recognize this ball?"*

All four kids recognized it immediately and one of them asked,

> *"How'd you get her ball, dad?"*

"Remember on the 15th hole when..." is how I started out.
At the end of the story, their jaws were all wide open in disbelief.

To say the least, they were mad.
Not me though.

I was glad to have an opportunity like this present itself when, in reality, it didn't mean that much.

I spoke to them, in detail, about what the ball represents.

In short, there were a few takeaways I hope they remember:

1. *You have to trust your partners, but that doesn't mean you don't verify along the way.*

2. *Cheating at golf is a slippery slope. The more you do it, the easier it becomes and the better you get. Some people are really good at this but you have to pay close attention.*

3. *Getting away with cheating doesn't make it right. Nor does it let you sleep well at night.*

4. *Doing the right thing even when no one is watching is still the right thing.*

5. *Sometimes mistakes happen (unintentional cheating) and people learn their lessons. If you realize you made a mistake later and 'got away with it' (happens to everyone in some form or fashion), learn the lesson instead of thinking about how you can try it again next time. Sometimes, these are the exact lessons you need to get better at whatever it is you're doing.*

6. *It's hard to believe in yourself if you win by cheating. I'd dare say it has the opposite effect on most people as their sub-conscious thoughts get the best of them and beat them in the end.*

7. *Cheating is a short-term strategy and is unsustainable. No matter what you're cheating in.*

8. *Cheating doesn't guarantee a win, but it does guarantee a personal loss of integrity. And that's not easy to replace, but it's possible.*

Unless you truly don't care or you've been taught that cheating is okay (in that case, all this is lost on you).

You see, golf is a lot like business.
In just about every business and industry there are truly good people and there are those who will cheat you.

On the surface, they all look the same.

The people who cheat in golf are more likely to have lots of practice bending rules and/or cheating people in one way or another in other areas of their lives.

They're good at it, and it's everywhere.

Sometimes it's within a company with reporting, statistics, invoices, terms and conditions, contracts, accounting.

Sometimes it's specific roles or titles such as cashiers, sales (in general), payroll managers, HR, hourly employees, CEOs, etc.

And sometimes it's just in general where people can hide and get away with it within religious organizations, hospitals, politics, media, phone companies, etc.

Is it everyone? **Absolutely NO!**
Is it in every industry? **Absolutely YES!**

It's not always easy to spot, but it's there...
I promise.

Have people—*as a whole*—learned to justify it by saying they have to make a living or that they're better than someone else in some way?
I believe they have.

Have we—*as a global society*—learned to accept that it's everywhere and lowered our standards instead of holding people accountable?
I believe we have.

I love seeing leaders take ownership of mistakes and accept their responsibility—especially those that don't give up immediately thereafter and they come back harder and faster the next time with a renewed sense of purpose as if to say,

"I learned my lesson and I'm better for it."

Conversely, I can't stand it when someone or some business blatantly —*and with confidence*—looks to cheat someone else and is more interested in what they can get now instead of building long-term relationships.

Bottom line for leaders is this.

Be alert, present and awake in all your dealings.
Trust people and businesses, but verify along the way.

And last, *intentional cheating is a self-defeating practice* that genuinely keeps players in all games and industries from ever truly reaching their full potential.

Be better, play hard, and win or lose with integrity—
No matter what game you're playing.

SECRET #46

The secret revealed is that the golf ball represents more than just a game; it serves as a lesson in character. This story also highlights the importance of honesty, even when no one is watching, and the enduring value of playing with integrity, both in sports and in business.

47

RIGHT HANDED VS. WRONG HANDED

O h how I wish education was a good way to gauge intelligence, work ethic, integrity, loyalty or anything else for that matter.

Please allow me a chance to elaborate.

Just over twenty years ago, I graduated with my MBA from USF. I remember, clearly, telling my wife that one of the most important lessons I learned is that I would **NEVER** hire someone nor promote them simply because they had a degree or certification.

What I saw very clearly was that some people were absolutely outstanding and worked their tails off, while others skated by, relied on Cliff's notes, other team members to pull their dead weight and complete bullcrap to get them through.

I worked with, listened to, and watched several people (certainly not all, but quite a few) go through the same exact program I did and I was appalled. I was beyond aggravated at how we'd all be MBAs and representing the school going forward with drastically different experiences, knowledge, and accountability.

I mean, really, we all had the same syllabus, lectures, classes, professors, and group projects but we were **NOT** the same. And from my understanding, it's like this in pretty much all schools and programs and that makes sense.

Why is this important?

It's important to understand because many people hear labels or titles such as MBAs or Dr. Such-n-Such or lawyers or accountants or scientists and immediately give them undue credit and think they're all the same.

Sorry to burst your bubble, but they're **NOT!**

Don't come at me. I didn't say they were all worthless. Not even close. I just said they're not all the same, and there's a distinct difference.

> *Every industry has leaders and followers.*
> *Multiple people can be leaders in a given industry and those same people can have vastly different views of the industry.*

One of my favorite examples of this are in healthcare. Some doctors do an amazing job of following what they've been taught and teaching others to do the same because that's the *"right way."* Others do an amazing job of maximizing profits while building practices that are bulletproof from a liability standpoint. Others have small practices where they spend more time with each of their patients and make sure everyone is seen and heard, regularly, and they have great bedside manners.

And then there are doctors who are into holistic medicine or natural healing and others who've gotten out of the business and now just want to help educate others.

Again, leaders, but different from the others.

Much different.

If you ask the same question to each of the *"leaders"* I just mentioned, you'll most likely get different answers from each.

> *How they see the data is different.*
> *How they interpret the data is different.*
> *What they use to measure or capture the data may be different.*
> *Their solutions will probably be different.*

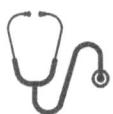 *Um, there's a reason we've all come to accept the phrase* ***"get a second opinion."***

Who's right?
What future are they considering?
Is money involved in their decision?
Do they really know what they're recommending?
Are they telling you what they were told to say or what you need to hear?
Are they trying to sell something else with their answer?
Do they really have your best interest at heart?

As leaders, reading people is **BIG**.

> *Sometimes it's people in your organization.*
> *Sometimes it's people you're hiring.*
> *Sometimes it's people in appointed positions.*
> *Sometimes it's your own doctor or people we follow on TV or in the media.*

My point is this:
There are **horrific** people in all industries and their titles and *education* are strikingly similar to those that are ***world-class.***

In other words, there's both **good and bad** and there's no good way to determine knowledge by looking at someone or merely seeing their name, titles, or degrees.

To be clear, there are **WILDLY** different opinions, viewpoints, perspectives, worldviews and end goals between professionals in the same industry—of almost every single industry.

So, why then, would we ever make major life decisions without consulting several professionals in a particular industry?

Should we consider the worst-case scenario?
Yes. But only if you're rational and it's explained well.

Should we consider the best-case option only?
No.

Should we ask lots of questions?
Undoubtedly.

Should we just trust the person right then and there because we're told everyone's doing it or everyone is buying it?

Here's the thing.

> Not everyone knows who or what's really behind anything anymore so it might be best to stop and take a good hard look around.

I'd say it's much closer to a **"hardly anyone really knows."**

Trust, but verify.
Retreat and retool.
Inquire and educate.
Explore the outer limits on thoughts.

Don't just take direction from those with titles.

Education is critical...
but **not in the title or degree or certification sense—**
it's in the knowledge and how it's used.

Some of the most knowledgable people I've ever met have no degree,
but lots of **common sense.**

In the **right hands**, education is an enabler that creates power:

> *The power to understand and make connections and know how and
>   when to use it.*
> *The power to understand problems and people and solve them.*
> *The power of knowing how to navigate and create solutions for the
>   greater good.*

In other words, **good intentions are magnified.**

In the wrong hands, education enables:

> *Corruption,*
> *Manipulation,*
> *Coercion,*
> *Greed,*
> *Abuse of power,*
> *Lies,*
> *Deceit... and*
> *Cover-ups.*

In other words, **bad intentions are magnified.**

Turns out, education merely brings out the best or worst in people—
just like titles, appointments, and leadership positions in every
industry out there.

If someone's earned their right to use their title or boast about their education, **you'll know it**. If not, **you'll know that too**.

Don't just put people on pedestals for education or titles until you determine if they're **"right"** handed or **"wrong"** handed.

And not just because of their educational background or title.

SECRET #47

The secret revealed is that education, titles, and certifications don't guarantee the quality or integrity of an individual. The true measure lies in how knowledge is applied, and blindly trusting someone based on their credentials can lead to disappointment, emphasizing the importance of critical thinking and evaluation in decision-making.

48

CHALLENGING YOURSELF

Turns out, the more you challenge yourself, the better you get... at everything.

As a leader, if you're not comfortable stepping out of your comfort zone, you're probably not growing as a person.

Doesn't matter your age.

Lessons are everywhere—it's just up to us to learn.

Learning is not something someone else does for us.

And, the more you learn, the more interesting your life becomes as it opens up new opportunities.

Whether you're starting a new school year, a new job, a new training program, or even just a new computer program, it's a great time for a reminder... for everyone.

Memorizing is not learning.
Busy work is not learning.
Getting good grades—*not learning.*

Learning does not require a school—

    Understanding is learning.
    Making mistakes is learning.
    Trying is learning.
    Asking questions is learning.

Learning increases knowledge—

    Knowledge betters the decision making process.
    And, decisions happen constantly throughout our days.

Don't be afraid to try new things and actually learn them.

You'll be surprised what kinds of things you'll enjoy that you never thought you would.

And, you'll inspire those that follow you to do more with their own lives.

And that is what being a leader is really about.

SECRET #48

The secret revealed is that continuous self-challenge leads to personal growth, and true learning is not confined to traditional educational settings but is found in embracing new experiences, making mistakes, and asking questions, ultimately enhancing decision-making and enriching life with unexpected joys.

49

CHECK VS. CHECKMATE

What's the right move?

Sometimes we're in situations where there's not a good solution.

A no-win scenario, of sorts.
All options seem like bad options, and they very well may be.

But, usually, one of the options is the best of the worst, better than the others. Less bad, or the least bad of the options.

Choose wisely.

Decision-making is often a dilemma in and of itself, but the thing is, *you have to choose.*

Not making a decision can actually be worse than deciding on one of the options.

I like to think of this in chess terms. If you've ever played chess you'll understand what I'm about to say.

And, with any luck, you'll resonate with the parallels.

CHECK *is very different than* ***CHECKMATE.***
CHECK requires analysis and complete focus.

All moves in your life prior to then led you to that point, but now, you have to make a decision.

If you don't, it's an eventual stalemate that could lead to *CHECKMATE* and game over.

You really shouldn't ignore CHECK.

First, though, understand that in real life we're all playing several different chess games, simultaneously—
And we have different opponents.

For most people, the goal is multi-dimensional: the goal is divided between not ending someone else's game and not allowing ours to be ended.

When another player's move requires our immediate attention in the form of *CHECK,* our focus leaves all the other boards.

The more time we spend in one board, the greater the chance other players will put you into *CHECK* on their interconnected board.

It's a vicious cycle, but one we can't ignore.

Sometimes we find ourselves in someone else's game that we've never met and they're on a mission to eliminate others.

We must always be aware of the potential and watch our own steps to ensure we're not blindsided in the form of *CHECK* or *CHECKMATE* by someone we didn't even know existed (more on this in a moment).

And, before I go any further, let me just say I wish I could have had this talk with four of my friends that are no longer a part of this world.

That said, this chapter encompasses many talks I *HAVE* had with other folks over the years where dire situations seemed insurmountable—but weren't.

Stay with me here—it's important.

And, if you know someone who might benefit from this message, please *SHARE* this chapter with them directly.

Okay, back to the game at hand.

CHECK says, "Okay, I have to get out of this mess immediately."

If you didn't recognize the struggle leading up to it you're more likely to repeat the problem, but that doesn't matter right now. You have to fix it, or at least address it to buy some time.

Sometimes you can get out of *CHECK* just by shifting other areas of your life and creating a block, of sorts.

Again, this buys you time.

Sometimes you lose a few of your pieces and you just have to cut your losses and move on.

And, if someone else gets you out of *CHECK* you need to pay extra close attention else you'll miss a great life lesson for sure.

And friends, the ultimate *CHECKMATE* in life results in the end of our game—literally.

Unfortunately, most people mistake *CHECK* for *CHECKMATE* and stress like it's the end of the world. They think they have no options, whereas usually there are many:

> *A shift to the left.*
> *A shift to the right.*
> *Bring in some assistance to block the threat— whatever.*

Sometimes you even have to change the rules to fit the game.

 Here's the thing though—every time you get out of CHECK, it should feel like a small win, even if you lose something in the battle.

If you reprogram your mind to think each of these losses are, in fact, a win, you'll find new ways to be okay with your decisions, both for the near-term and the long-term.

Speaking of our decisions—

We all know that stress clouds our judgment and vision—and, sure, it may feel like we're trapped, but that's rarely true.

Reasons for bad decisions are many, but what's needed now is some type of decision. Preferably, the **lesser of two evils.**

> *Someone holding a gun to your head is a potential CHECKMATE (you probably didn't even known you were playing with them).*
> *Losing your legs in a car accident is CHECK.*
> *Not having enough money to buy a new car? CHECK.*
> *A car that breaks down and you don't have money to fix it yet. CHECK.*
> *An overdose that lands you in a hospital but doesn't kill you. CHECK.*
> *A jail sentence and then a release, CHECK.*
> *An addiction of some type that's bringing you to your knees. CHECK.*
> *Depression that starts affecting your daily life. CHECK.*

> *Someone breaking up with you or cheating may feel like*
> *CHECKMATE, but it's an easy CHECK.*

Anything money-related is fixable.
Again, it may not be your best option, but there are options.
Heck, bankruptcy's an option if you really need it.
But, yes, everything money-related is *CHECK*.

You have to keep going.

Along those same lines, *CHECK* can be found in jobs, relationships, and in family life.

> *Hate your job or lose it unexpectedly? CHECK.*
> *In an abusive relationship of some type? CHECK. (This is a bit trickier*
> *to recognize unless it's physical.)*
> *Have toxic people in your life, perhaps other family members?*
> *CHECK.*
> *Survived a suicide attempt? CHECK.*

It's okay to change your situation *(I'd dare say it's necessary)* and make things better for yourself. Don't feel bad about this. It's not being selfish if you truly feel like you're in *CHECK*.

You just have to be **self-aware** and **honest with yourself.**

And no, I'm not downplaying *CHECK* at all, nor does this relate to the old saying of *"keeping everything in check."*

CHECK, in all these situations is a time to buckle down and dig your way out—

> *Get scrappy if you need to, in a resourceful way.*
> *Get help if necessary.*
> *Fight like hell!*

Life coaches are a "thing" for a reason, just make sure they're on your team.

And yes, *CHECK* is a mindset and it's relative to you and your current situation and resources. It can be all-consuming to some and a shrug of the shoulders to others.

It's important to know yourself and understand your **modus operandi** when stressed.

You can practice potential scenarios and think them through. You can even use the saying *"You better CHECK yo'self, before you WRECK yo'self!"* I interpret that as a way to prepare for the known and do you best to anticipate the unknowns.

Related to the unknowns—keep in mind, some circumstances are beyond our control and we cannot possibly be prepared for everything life throws our way.

As for what to do when in *CHECK*, there's no right answer as long as there's some action taken.

Suffice it to say, inaction is a detriment.

Think of it as being in the middle of a room that's on fire on all four walls. You *HAVE* to do something.

In chess, they call this **ZUGZWANG**—essentially where you're forced to move and no matter what you do you'll be put at a disadvantage. You can't just skip your turn (or do nothing).

Ultimately, *CHECK* brings great awareness where maybe there was none prior.

And yes, all leaders will be in *CHECK* at some point in their lives. Heck, some of us, many times (me with my hand raised).

We may not always like our options, **but we have options.**

And yes, in case you're still not clear, doing nothing *IS* an option—but a *CHECK* left unchecked often gets worse and can be devastating in the right circumstances. *Think:*

> *Health issues,*
> *Check engine lights,*
> *Tire pressure warnings,*
> *Violent behavior that's escalating,*
> *Or, perhaps, that burning room I just mentioned.*

Ironically, by ignoring some of these small checks, they turn into the *BIG CHECKS,* monetarily (that was the spin you saw in your head but couldn't place until this moment).

So, yes, options to get out of *CHECK* require movement or action of some type—

> *It might include selling something at a loss after investing heavily,*
> *which sucks—but it's an option.*
> *It might involve losing a friend that constantly drags you down.*
> *It might involve getting a lower-paying job.*

It's nothing more than a reset or a setback, but it's not *CHECKMATE.*

Resilience is critical in life. *And yes, we all have problems—*
and sometimes we cringe and just have to go a different direction in order to get back on track.

The rebound is where it's at.

And, no, I'm not talking about hooking up with that one person you can't stand but, heck, tonight, any port in the storm will do.

I'm talking about when you've hit some type of bottom in the form of a *CHECK,* it's important to go on the offensive. You have to!

The lesson here is that you'll need to dial up your intensity and find a way to go up a level on your growth spiral.

Else, you're destined to find yourself in a constant *"check-fest"* and you'll forever feel like you're scrambling while slowly sliding backwards.

Again, *CHECK* is usually solvable—but you have to get back to a position where you can focus on all the other pieces. In other words, you have to get out of *CHECK* as quickly as you can.

Your life is your game and you control the pieces. Make your move and let others make theirs.

> *And, this is a good time to remind you that everyone else is playing chess with their lives and **you never know** when you'll be playing them or what the consequences of our decisions will really bring.*

Why? Well, it's mostly that our lives are full of complicated choices and the data we use to interpret—*or that's even available to us*—is never perfect nor complete.

Meaning, we're dealing with imperfect data sets to aid us.

Fun, huh? Well, that's life.

And, to further illustrate this, the players we're playing with are always changing their own strategy *OR* the board they're playing on.

Sometimes their strategy is merely to stay alive and other times they're coming at you with everything they've got to eliminate *YOU* from the game—or at least knock you off of *THEIR* board.

You have to be able to learn and recognize who the players are and at what level they're playing.

Some people are sneaky and require constant attention where you just can't catch a break as you're always on the defense and dealing with *CHECK... and then others let you play peacefully and worry about other players' boards, sometimes even offering strategy support or assists.*

Know the difference.

Life lessons are easy to find if you're looking—and we all learn at different rates and at different times.

CHECK *means you're still in the game and life's just that—a game.*
    And it's a game worth playing.
CHECKMATE *is inevitable at some point, but not now, not today.*

Get your head in the game and play on—even if it means taking the pieces you have left and starting over somewhere else.

It's your move, chief!

SECRET #49

The secret revealed is that life is a complex game of chess with constant challenges (CHECK) that demand thoughtful action. While facing difficulties, the key is to understand that CHECK is not CHECKMATE, and with resilience and strategic moves, one can navigate through life's intricate board, always staying in the game.

50

BIOMETRICALLY SPEAKING

see what you did there.

And now, with a great degree of certainty, I can predict what you'll do next.

I know this because I have all your data. I know what you've reacted to, what you've taken action on, what you like, what turns you off, what makes you smile, and what causes disgust.

Biometrics are incredible like that.

Years ago, Google introduced heat maps for analyzing websites. Impressively, once you used the plugin, you could see everything that happened on a webpage. You could see where people clicked, how long they were on the page, where their attention went, etc.

You'd get true *hot spots.*

It was a game-changer. Before, it was a guessing game. Once heat-mapping was introduced, you could fine tune just about anything and watch the impact—good or bad. You could do A-B testing on the frontend or split-testing altogether and really fine tune your results.

Or, you could simply change your live site and watch changes in real-time. Change colors on call-to-action buttons and watch clicks come in or clicks stop, completely. Change where an item is on a page and drastically impact how many people interact with it. If you had things *"above the fold,"* it was much more likely to be seen. Below, and it had no chance.

Most of this was before all the smart phones were introduced. Desktops, laptops, and tablets ruled the traffic.

That all changed.

Now, heat mapping technologies have moved to our phones as well as everyday products, and they're based on our eyes as well as our faces. Eye-tracking, facial analysis, and electrodermal activity is all captured.

Where we look, how long, and what we're focusing on is all mapped out. What our expressions are, how we react, and what they mean is tracked. And this is all well and good... until it isn't.

More on that in a minute.

Oh, and you know that forward facing camera on your phone that's looking right at you while you scroll? Yeah, well, there's something you should know.

Remember that old song by The Police called, "Every Breath You Take"? —If you look at the lyrics you'll have a good idea as to what your phone is collecting.

Really, take a look.

From a pure marketing perspective, this kind of data is gold. It's gold because it results in money—lots of it. For everyone who fine-tunes their product offering.

The more a business can utilize these technologies the easier it is to influence their customers and change their behaviors.

The more marketers know, the more they manipulate variables and get people to take actions. The more they get people to take action, the more they want to do more—to get more.

From a leadership perspective, this creates a challenge—

> *How much is too much?*
> *How far is too far?*
> *Ethically, is there a line we have to draw?*
> *What if we find ways of completely manipulating the human*
>   *experience and we use it for the wrong reasons?*

It's all there.
It's a perfect storm just waiting to happen.
Especially if we allow AI to choose what we do with the information.

In other words... if we take human emotion out—
It's easy to use everything we find out *to our advantage.*

But, do we?

Do we want to create an environment where we capture everything, at all times, and under every circumstance?

Do we want to be able to manipulate *every variable* and change our offerings for each person so we can sell them some new thing or get them to take whatever action we want to?

Again, on paper, it makes sense. But in real-life we have to stand up for humanity and say no.

We have have stopping points and hold each other accountable.

We have to allow people to just be people and live their lives without being tracked everywhere.

 *Otherwise, WE become the target. WE become the hunted. WE become a mere statistic—and WE lose.*
All of us. As a whole.

Leaders, think about future generations—

Your children. Your children's children.
We have to be able to allow free will, freedom of choice, and freedom of expressions.

It all matters.

Else, we're setting ourselves up for a complete takeover from those at the top who can control it all at the push of a button.

There has to be a point where we stop measuring.
Where we stop collecting.
Where we stop trying to get more out of everyone.

> **If true leadership is about leading people—**
> **Then where we lead them matters.**

Let's make sure we lead our teams with ethical boundaries relating to biometrics and other invasive technologies that make sense—
not just dollars.

SECRET #50

This chapter underscores the power and potential ethical challenges of biometric data collection. The extensive information that can be gathered from individuals through technologies like eye-tracking and facial analysis is highlighted, emphasizing its value in marketing. However, a cautionary tone is introduced, questioning the ethical limits of data manipulation and stressing the need for leaders to establish boundaries to protect individuals' privacy and preserve humanity in the face of advancing technology.

51

TOXICITY

Hurricane victims know first hand what water damage creates. Not just the day it happens, but the next week. And two weeks after. And a month after that.

Toxic chemicals, toxic waste, and toxic mold all get out of hand over time if you don't take care of them. They spread. They make everything around them worse.

Toxic behaviors are the same. Heck, toxic masculinity and toxic femininity are both hot topics in society right now because of how many people they affect.

But there's another one.

One that doesn't get the publicity of the others. One that doesn't make the headlines nor many of the viral videos because of how sexy or cool it is.

Because it's not.

It's toxic employees.

They come in all shapes and sizes and varying levels of toxicity, but they're all similar in the damage they cause.

As leaders, it's important to recognize—

What toxic behavior is,
How it spills over to the work environment, and
How it affects other employees, customers, and the company's
brand overall.

More so, leaders need to know how to handle toxic employees to ensure damage is minimized.

More on that, shortly.

 *Toxic behavior in a work environment can be simplified by saying it's a person who causes some type of distress to others by their negative habits, behaviors, or ongoing actions.*

Now, this is tricky because everyone has something they do that someone else doesn't like. *We don't get to just point out every negative thing and say that person's toxic.*

There has to be trends. Behaviors that are consistent. Habits that are subtle, but noticed. A couple examples include—

Someone who's continuously negative or a pessimist, in general.
Someone who procrastinates every time work is assigned to them and waits until the last possible moment to take action.

Or, someone who says yes all the time and doesn't add anything constructive. If you recall, this is also known as a **disaffiliate.**

What about **insubordination** and **sabotage?**

Someone who just refuses to follow along and makes things harder for the team, in general.

Yep, huge problem.

What if someone is continuously disrespectful? *It takes its toll.*

There are others, too.

Folks who never take responsibility for anything.
Those who always want to work *alone* and have no interest in others.
Those who love to *gossip* and bring drama to every conversation or meeting.

And what about clock watchers?
You know, those only interested in being there to get paid and are ready to dip the second their shift is up regardless of their work being done.

There's more.

Those who constantly make excuses and pawn their work off on other people. Or, perhaps, it's the person that harasses others and makes the environment difficult to work in because they know it all and no one can do it as good as them.

Here's what happens—

> *These people drag others down.*
> *They make the rest of the team dread going to work.*
> *Often, when left unvetted, others on the team end up leaving.*
> *Morale drops overall and the company culture is affected.*

As leaders, protecting your team is vital.

Sometimes, this means you have to protect them from *someone on the inside.*

It's never easy, but it's important.

And, this may surprise you, but the answer is **not to simply remove** the toxic person.

Depending on how your team is set up there are a number of different steps that can be taken.

1. *Hold team meetings where positive traits are reinforced and praised openly to help with the company's culture.*

2. *Offer resources and encourage team members to participate in online courses, counseling, and professional development.*

3. *Ensure company policies and procedures are clear about what behaviors are and are not acceptable. *Legally speaking, it's necessary as you move towards any disciplinary actions.*

4. *Speak directly with the employee about what the concern is, the effect it's having on the team or the company, and what can be done immediately to make positive changes.*

Often, people are blatantly unaware of their behaviors and how they affect others. Once they understand and are given the opportunity to make positive changes, many people do.

Turning a toxic employee into a brand champion takes a special kind of leader, but it happens regularly.

The alternative is to simply remove the toxicity from the team.
This is necessary when a leader has exhausted all other resources and decides the best course of action is to go separate ways.

You see, being a leader doesn't mean everyone will follow along.
It doesn't mean everyone will like your decisions.
It doesn't mean everyone will play nicely.

It does, however, mean you have a team of people who depend on you.
It means others trust *YOU* to do what's right for the team.

It means you have to put the team first and take care of those you're leading.

When you discover toxicity, it's worth exploring—

Where it's coming from,
Who it's going to, and
What'll happen if you let it grow.

A leader worth following will **nip toxic behaviors early** and guide his or her team towards a positive work environment.

And, it **only happens** when the leader is *paying attention* to the little things and *truly cares* about everyone on the team.

Be that kind of leader.

SECRET #51

The secret revealed is that toxic employees can be as destructive as other forms of toxicity in life. Recognizing and addressing negative behaviors within a team is crucial for maintaining a positive work environment. Effective leaders don't just remove toxic individuals; they employ strategies such as reinforcing positive traits, offering resources for personal development, clarifying company policies, and directly addressing concerns with the employee to foster positive change. Being a leader requires safeguarding the team AND prioritizing their well-being, even if it means making tough decisions to ensure a healthy work culture.

52

SELF-LOVE

An interesting discussion about self-love took place in our house recently.

It started with me basically saying you have to love yourself before you can love others. It ended with me talking about the leadership element.

I mean, really, what does *"love yourself"* mean?
And what is *"self love"* anyway?

Well, the answer is one that really applies to everyone—
and is foundational to things like self-esteem, self confidence, and certainly, self-respect.

In a way, they're correlated.

Doesn't matter if you're 10, 12, 15, 16, 25, 50, 75, or 100—
These things matter.

Self-love essentially says you're taking care of **YOU** in as many different ways you can in order to give, fully, to others (i.e., to be a leader).

You know how in airplanes they tell adults to put their oxygen masks on *FIRST* and then take care of children around you? Well, the concept here is strikingly similar.

If you put yourself first, and take care of *YOU*, it's easier to give your best self to others.

If you find yourself taking care of others *FIRST*, you're often depleted and have no energy to take care of yourself at the end of the day.

I sometimes find myself in this rut and I have to hit *RESET* and pull myself out.

It's a slippery slope.

 So, what kinds of "take care of yourself" are we talking here?

Great question. A high level look would include three pieces:

> *Inputs,*
> *Maintenance, and*
> *Outputs*

Each one would then have several *sub-topics.*

Here's some examples...

Inputs would include things that go into your body: *food, liquids, air, nature, conversations with trusted advisors and friends, reading, media, chemicals, substances, hygiene products, learning, building skills, what we see, sounds, lighting, etc.*

Maintenance would include: *sleep, exercise, stretching, clothing, mindfulness, cleanliness of both your personal and immediate environment, setting boundaries, setting goals, commitments, being* responsible, integrity, accountability, bringing your passions with you, personal grooming, gratitude, practicing skills, self-protection, security, friendship, resourcefulness, creativity, laughter, measuring progress against baselines, self-assessments, achievement, empathy, coping, self-talk, checking your work, feedback loops, community support systems, finding and/or going to your "happy place," etc.

Outputs would include: speaking, writing, singing, dancing, art, manners, giving to others, respect for others, showing up, new experiences, acceptance, celebrating successes, sharing, contributing, expressing emotions, etc.

> The more you know, understand, and take care of yourself,
> the easier it is to **move forward** and **lead by example** with an
> **air of confidence** and **authenticity** that is not easily shaken.
> It's about valuing yourself and understanding your own self-worth.

Please note, an air of confidence is **NOT** the same as having an inflated sense of oneself or arrogance.

When taken to extremes, the value of oneself and one's own importance over everyone else's leads to narcissism.

Also, this isn't the same as being self-centered. That's when everything is about you and not about others, at all.

Think of the sub-topics as stepping stones.

They all lead to a path of self-love. Each one needs to be looked at individually, in some capacity, and considered regularly as you go through life.

Not all at once, but they all matter in the scheme of things and almost all of them relate to choices we make.

In other words, we, for the most part, get to choose our own paths, but they're made up of many small steps.

And, if we spend too much time on any one of the small steps, as in, if we do nothing but read or exercise or dance, we suffer major imbalances and consequences overall.

 *Maslow's hierarchy of needs suggests a pyramid that starts with basic needs as the foundation and works its way all the way up to self-actualization.*

Self-actualization is really not far off from self-love and isn't a *"I finally made it!"* type of destination.

It's an ongoing ebb and flow of life where we feel like we have some semblance of control one minute and then feel a bit off-balance the next.

And you know what else is at the top of the pyramid relating to self-love? **Discipline.**

It's ignoring that flashy thing in front of you right now in the hopes of getting something better later on.

Discipline shows how committed you are to your dreams and aspirations, especially on days when you just want to quit.

Your discipline, today, keeps yesterday's promises so the future you can reap the benefits.

The more we can take care of for ourselves though, the easier it becomes to deal with external influences in a rational manner that provides value to the people who follow us—instead of being a burden or a victim.

Clearly, self-love and leadership are married at the hip.

And, since everyone's out there playing *"follow the leader"* anyway, it's best we take care of ourselves and *give them a leader worth following.*

SECRET #52

The secret revealed is that self-love is the foundation for personal well-being, leadership, and positive influence on others. By prioritizing self-care in various aspects of life, individuals can navigate challenges, maintain balance, and authentically lead with confidence, creating a positive impact on those around them.

53

THE PROBLEM

Now that's a problem worth solving!

I love that line. It says so much without saying much at all.

Solving problems is how I spend most of my time so it's no surprise when new problems surface.

As a matter of fact, it's expected.
And, it's where I get the most satisfaction.

Truth is, we all have problems. Like, everyone (no exceptions).

Problems aren't the problem. Solutions are.

How we solve problems *today* has everything to do with
what problems we solve tomorrow.

If we take shortcuts, chances are we'll get to repeat the same problem
again... And again... And again.

If we solve it but don't get it completely right we'll get to redo it at some point. *Maybe not tomorrow, but definitely in the near future.*

If we get the solution right by doing a bit of *homework*, it has a lasting effect.

This applies to problems in most areas of our lives:

> *Parenting, home repairs, auto repairs, finances, learning, sports, plumbing, coaching, customer service, building businesses, politics, food, sickness, etc.*

You can't avoid problems, but your
> **approach to solving them shapes the life you'll get to lead.**

Again—

You can't avoid problems, but your
> **approach to solving them shapes the life you'll get to lead.**

And, as a leader, I can't stress enough how important this next concept is.

If you want to have interesting problems—*or what some call good problems*—take the time to solve the little everyday ones.

Else, they'll haunt you the rest of your life.

Look in the mirror and start with the question:

> **"What's your problem?"**

Dig deep and focus on solving one little problem at a time.
The "small problems" are where it's at.
The day-to-day crap a lot of people avoid.

Every time you solve one of these problems, you immediately have an increase in satisfaction.

You build connections of **hows** and **whys.** You slowly piece together the world around you.

Your self confidence increases.
Your belief in yourself gets a little stronger.
Your self-reliance gets a much-needed boost.

Whether it's in your business, on your team, in your data, at home, or in a classroom—**the more problems you solve at the ground level, the better you become, at everything.**

Once you get through those *everyday* hurdles you'll be much better equipped for the next level.

Think of it like a video game:

> *You have to solve "THE PROBLEM" at this level to get to the next level.*

Now, if you always pass your problems over to someone else, you're making your life *WAY* more difficult as you're missing out on valuable skills and lessons that will help you in the future.

Be a problem solver and you'll get more out of life.

You won't have fewer problems—
You'll just have problems you look forward to solving.

SECRET #53

The secret revealed is that problem-solving is a skill and one that's critical for leaders. Problems aren't the problem, solutions are, and the more experience leaders get with solving day-to-day problems, the easier it is to tackle more interesting problems. Get comfortable with the question, "What's your problem?" and get immense satisfaction out of knowing you have what it takes to solve it. The more problems you solve, the more interesting your problems become.

54

THE MOVIE

Oh man.
Not five minutes into it and I knew.
My heart slowed down a bit.
My breaths were deeper and longer.
My mind wandered.

I felt like I had just gone back in time.
Like I was sitting with an old friend.

Words and ideas that changed my life.
Thoughts that made me question my own.
Concepts that made lasting impressions.

For real.
My cogitation button had just been pressed.

It was a movie I'd first see when I was thirteen.
I'd see it again at age seventeen and again at twenty-one.
Each time I watched, it meant something different.

All of a sudden I was twenty-four.
I was working as a front end manager in a Target and knee-deep into my MBA program where the movie showed up again.

But, this time, it was different.

It was a class in the Leadership tract.
Specifically, this class was on Servant Leadership.
We had deep-dives every. single. week.

And I mean **DEEP.**

Somewhere around week five, we were assigned a ten page essay.
To break down and dissect the specific elements of leadership from one of four different movies.

 That week we re-watched this movie individually, as a team, and then about ten more times as we started, stopped, paused, rewound and fast-forwarded our way through it all.

DVD players were still new and we certainly didn't have one yet.
This was all on VHS.

It just hit different this time.

For the first time I saw how impactful someone's voice could be—

As a teacher.
As a person who gets others to think.
As someone who truly cared about others.
As someone who saw that helping others was more important than
   following "the crowd."

It connected. Deeply.
To the point where I was truly inspired.

Two weeks later I had quit my job and decided I was going to make a difference somewhere.

I was going to do it my way and not join in the *"lock step"* of life.

Everyone thought I was crazy, but I followed through.

It was true,

"Words and ideas CAN change the world."

And last night, when watching it again with my thirteen-year-old, it all came full-circle.

I remembered the things that changed because of that movie.

I remembered—

> *The feelings.*
> *The decisions.*
> *The raw emotions.*
> *The influences on my thoughts over the years.*
> *The way I taught classes.*
> *The questions I asked.*
> *The way I've tried to look at things differently.*

And just how many times over the years I've used bits and pieces and quotes from it.

Maybe you've seen it?
Maybe it impacted you the same way?

Or, maybe you have your own movie that's done something like this for you?

I mean, really, they say we're all shaped by the things we see, hear, and feel, and this movie was a major contributor to my life.

What movie?

Well, I can only hope that when my real-life movie ends, it'll be with those I've influenced standing up on their desks and saying:

"O Captain! My Captain!"

SECRET #54

Inspiration can come from a myriad of sources—books, videos, reels, podcasts, conversations, and even movies. What we put into our mind matters and the power of narratives should never be underestimated. Words and ideas can, in fact, change the world if put together in the right order at the right time. It's important to find your own way in the world and help others find theirs. That's what leadership is really about.

55

THE TALK

Not long ago I had a talk with one of my daughters. It was after hearing a number of her excuses for not getting her work done.

It wasn't the first time so I wanted to ensure she understood a few things as she'll soon be in the workforce. And, though the talk was with her, the content applies to everyone.

From a leadership perspective, it's important to understand what is said here and own it. Everyone on your team should hear it as well as your team is an extension of you... Heck, your own children may benefit from it as well.

"THE TALK" as it's called here is *one that's worth having.*

> *Concepts that are worth exploring.*
> *Thoughts that are worth thinking.*
> *Ideas that are worth sharing.*

We all have things we struggle with, but it's up to each of us to use them to our advantage.

Here's *"THE TALK"* as it happened:

So what you're white. So what you're black. So what you're hispanic. So what you have ADHD. So what your relative was a slave owner. So what you have relatives that were slaves. So what you're from another country. So what you believe or don't believe in God. So what you have a disability. So what you have a PhD or if you dropped out of school. So what you have a Tesla. So what you're a billionaire. So what you do or don't drink alcohol. So what you still wear a mask. So what you have a tattoo or piercings. So what you're a girl. So what if you're older or younger. So what if you're heavier or more fit. So what if you like those in the same sex, opposite sex or no one at all. So what if you have a 3.0, a 4.0 or were the valedictorian.

SO WHAT!

Oh, don't get me wrong. I care. But I don't.

If we're here to work, then let's work.
If we're on a team together, then let's help each other.
If we have a common goal, let's get at it.
If we have to depend on each other *(and we do),* then be dependable in a way that matters.

Don't expect special treatment because **YOU** think you're special.

Today, when you show up—*show up.* Bring the you that deserves to be there. Make sure others know you're there because you can hold your own or help in a way that others need.

You.
Not the story book version of you.
Not the online version of you on Instagram.
Not the legend of you.
You.

If you can't show up and perform without a caveat, that's on you. Mirrors are cheap and everywhere for a reason.

If it takes leveling up or shoring up skills, then that's something you can choose. If it's something where you can actually improve based on knowledge or skills, then make it happen.

And, remember, progress over perfection. Just keep getting better.

If, instead, you're competing on age, weight, beauty, strength, or something else you can't much control, move to something else.

While it's important to accept others, it's also important to **NOT** allow these things to lower expectations of teams or companies just because.

Too many people get into teams or jobs and then blame some *"thing"* for their inability to keep up with those that are leading or performing at a higher level. Then, they spend their time trying to justify their inadequacies and insecurities instead of improving in any form or fashion.

The problem is, it leaks out. It spills over to teammates that then lose motivation. It creates a toxic work environment. It works its way out to customers. It reflects poorly on the team output or product line. It degrades relationships all around and people start working their way out of your life.

 It's not them, it's you.
It's the story of you you're telling.

You see, we all have access to education *(don't mistake school and college for education)*. We all have access to information. We all have access to tools that can make our lives better.

We all have far better resources available to us than at any other point in history, but we have to be willing to do something with it.

And, you have to be accountable to yourself.

The version of you *today* may not be what you want, but it's what you have. The version of you *a month from now* is completely up to you. The version of you *next year* is potentially so different that you wouldn't even recognize it.

And yet, many people feel stuck unnecessarily.

We all have to play the cards we were dealt.

All that said, we all have millions of choices as to how we play, where we play, who we play with, and what we're playing for.

Everybody's better than you at something and you're better than everybody at something as well.

> **Humility** *says we can accept when someone's better at something,*
> **Resilience** *says we deal with it,*
> **Wisdom** *says we look for ways to improve instead of thinking we have no way forward, and*
> **Gratitude** *says we're thankful for the opportunity to even try.*

So, instead of believing your own story of why you *can't* do something, dig deep and find a way to get in the game.

Prove to yourself and others that you can, in fact, do anything.

And, when you do, others get to use **YOU** as the example that made things happen—and they'll use all of your previous *excuses* as your *advantage* instead.

So, go on...

Make your advantage happen!

SECRET #55

In a world teeming with labels and preconceptions, true value lies not in one's background or identity but in one's actions and commitment. Whether you're from a privileged background or face personal challenges, the essence is in showing up genuinely and contributing meaningfully. Rather than leaning on excuses or external factors, the key is self-accountability, continuous improvement, and embracing opportunities. The real game-changer is not the story you've been handed but the narrative you choose to create and live by, proving that personal growth and achievement are within everyone's grasp.

THE SECRET TAKEAWAY

The 55 Leadership Secrets revealed in this book have the potential to transform you into one of the best leaders out there, bar none. You now possess what very few leaders do—the understanding and value of what's inside of you and how to give others something worth following.

As such, here's a quick takeaway of what's in your toolkit so you can proudly wear your *"best leader"* badge with honor.

The best leaders aren't the ones out there barking orders at their teams nor the ones micromanaging every second of the day.

Instead, they're out there setting up their team for success, paying attention to the little things, and finding a way to make things happen regardless of obstacles.

The best leaders are serving their teams as though they're the most important part of the equation... because they are. Mutual respect for self and all others is critical in their day-to-day dealings and they regularly trust, but verify.

They also know when enough is enough, the best ways to communicate messages, and that we don't really **KNOW** much at all.

The best leaders are making sure their people get the specialized training they need and have the right tools for the job. They know the difference between delegation and empowerment, being right handed and wrong handed, and winning and being a winner.

They also know the difference between a victim's mindset and a captain's mindset, as well as check and checkmate.

The best leaders make sure their people have drinks before they need them, and food before they're starving. They look for root causes, system failures, and they don't grade on a curve.

You know what else?

The best leaders are comfortable with being uncomfortable. They embrace the feelings that come with challenging themselves, welcoming others, *AND* the importance of resilience.

The best leaders embrace the idea of growth spirals, use the WGMGI model, and understand, fully, that you must be present to win.

The best leaders understand loyalty, how to navigate life's kayak with precision, and are impressive, even when empty handed. *They compliment others, use all their senses wisely, and let people be heard.*

The best leaders know that leadership is not a title and that one's position doesn't make one a leader. They understand toxicity, the difference between leaders, followers and disaffiliates, and why ethical decisions are so critical for the future of humanity.

The best leaders aren't the ones with the most money, or education, *they're the ones* that make the biggest impact. They're the ones that make us all feel seen, heard, and loved. They're the ones that create the ripples that have the far-reaching effects.

So, get out there and lead with *both purpose AND passion while you find a way to make it happen.* I see your struggles, but I also see how you're using them to your advantage.

And, that's it, my friend.

Thanks for allowing me to go on this journey with you and for trusting *ME* to help *YOU* piece it all together. I look forward to hearing great things about you and *following your lead* in the future.

Best of successes!

WHAT COMES NEXT

You've just spent the last several hours (perhaps days or weeks) building something important—your leadership mindset, your strategy, and your belief in what's possible.

Now it's time to do something with it.

Start small.
Start strong.
Start somewhere.

Whether it's how you show up tomorrow, how you coach your team, how you raise your kids, or how you handle your toughest conversation—you have a choice.

You can lead.

And no, it won't always be easy.

But you've seen how powerful leadership can be when it's built on trust, clarity, courage, and care.

You've got tools now. A system. Language. Stories that matter.
And a whole new way to look at the people around you.

So what comes next?

You do.

PASS IT ON

Leadership multiplies when it's shared.

When you *live* what you've learned...
When you *model* what you believe...
When you *teach* what you've seen work...

You give someone else permission to lead too.

So pass it on—

The moment that meant the most to you,
The concept you keep coming back to,
The part that changed something inside of you,
The secret that connected like no other.

Share it. Teach it. Talk about it.

Maybe it's with your team. Maybe it's with your family. Maybe it's in the form of a review online. Maybe it's a post to your friends on social media. *Maybe it's with someone who doesn't see themselves as a leader... yet.*

This is how a single book becomes a legacy.

And if this book spoke to you, *the hope is you'll speak up for it.*

And there's more where that came from—
More moments, more movement, more tools—
Just search my name and step into your *"next chapter."*

A FINAL WORD

You made it.

Not just to the end of a book, but to the *start of something new.*

Leadership isn't about being perfect. It's about caring about your people. Being intentional. Showing up. Trying again. Being the kind of person others want to follow—and knowing what to do when they do.

Thank you for trusting me with your time, your attention, and your leadership journey.

It's been an honor to walk with you through these pages.

I hope something in this book becomes your go-to when life gets loud, when decisions feel hard, or when someone you care about needs you at your best.

Until we meet again, keep showing up. Keep noticing the good. Keep creating the moments. Keep leading in the unique way only you can.

I wish you the best, always.

With gratitude,

Shawn Trautman

(To learn more about Shawn, check the final page.)

ABOUT SHAWN

Shawn Trautman leads by example—*and sometimes by accident.*

He's held nearly every leadership role you can imagine—*coach, CEO, trainer, planner, team lead, supervisor, manager, operations director*—and dozens that never came with a title. He's helped organizations grow, people level up, and teams find their rhythm.

His career started on the dance floor, where he taught thousands how to move with confidence. Since then, he's worked in *corporate leadership, sports coaching, systems consulting, entrepreneurship, education, and government operations.*

Each role added to the systems and secrets you now hold in this book.

Shawn is also the author of several books including:

> *Cherry Picking the Good, (Finding the Good),*
> *The Power of Moments (Making it Matter),* and
> *Picture Yourself Dancing (Starting Something New).*

He's also the creator of the *VECTOR Performance System* and more than 50 full-length instructional videos.

His work is about more than performance.
It's about connection, character, and purpose—and helping people show up as leaders worth following in the moments that matter most.

He believes real leadership isn't measured by titles, but by the lives you touch—and the moments when you help others rise.
That's the legacy he's chasing.
And if this book found its way into your hands, maybe you are too.

www.ingramcontent.com/pod-product-compliance
Lightning Source LLC
Chambersburg PA
CBHW070910120626
46546CB00001B/208